The Territorial Seed Company

GARDEN COOKBOOK

Homegrown Recipes for Every Season

Edited by Lane Morgan

Sasquatch Books

Seattle, Washington

Design by Jane Jeszeck
Cover and interior illustration by Jonathan Combs

Library of Congress Cataloging-in-Publication Data

The Territorial seed company garden cookbook : homegrown recipes for every
   season / edited by Lane Morgan
      p. cm.
         Includes index.
         ISBN 0-912365-40-4 : $9.95
         1. Cookery. I. Morgan, Lane. 1949-
TX714.T47 1991   90-27660
641.5—dc20   CIP

Sasquatch Books
1931 Second Avenue
Seattle, WA 98101

Contents

....

Margaret Abplanalp, Portland, OR
Deanne Adams, Vancouver, WA
Lorry Alsip, West Linn, OR
Jane Ammerman, Eugene, OR
Diana Anderson, Enumclaw, WA
Nikki Anderson, Wauna, WA
Debbie Arney, Olympia, WA
Jane Baier-Nelson, Shaw
  Island, WA
Janice Baker, Eugene, OR
Ruth Barnes, Sequim, WA
Margot Becker, Snohomish, WA
Jane Becklake, Saltspring
  Island, BC
Don and Evelyn Belloff, Friday
  Harbor, WA
Cheryl Boden, Union Gardens,
  Hillsboro, OR
Alice Bond, Lyons, OR
Janet Boyce, Ellensburg, WA
Alice Boyet, Crescent City, CA
Bob Brooks, Seattle, WA
Jan Brown, Clinton, WA
Robert Brown, Hillsboro, OR
Lois M. Burrow, Seaford, DE
Rosa Chapman, Wildwood, CA
Jan Cole, Pittsburg, CA
Suzy Cook, Bainbridge Island, WA
Carol Danz, Harmony Farm, Cave
  Junction, OR
Jan Davis, Calistoga, CA
Sarah Davis, Portland, OR
Donna Dreessen, Port
  Orchard, WA
Paul Dreykus, Shelton, WA
Jana Drobinsky, El Cerrito, CA
Audrey Edmonds, Poulsbo, WA
Freida Fenn, Port Townsend, WA
Aaron Flier, Pacifica, CA
J.P. Frances, Mustang, OK
Maxine Fritz, Canby, OR
Margie Fromherz, Salem, OR
E. Fuller, Portland, OR
Lina Gallagher, Seattle, WA
Iola Garrett, Azalea, OR
Vicky Giannangelo, Friday
  Harbor, WA
Norma Dolowitz Giddings,
  Petaluna, CA
Sandra Gilbert, Marysville, WA
Debra Gillis-Berlin, Astoria, OR
Marian Glenz, Meyers Chuck, AK
Sylvia Goheen, Olympia, WA
Lois Golik, Woodland, WA
Sky Groth, Emeryville, CA
June Hadland, Chehalis, WA
Carl Hanscam, Occidental, CA
Laura Hartmore, Snohomish, WA
Margaret Hedin, Port
  Angeles, WA
Joan Hogan, Albany, OR
Kay Holland, Poulsbo, WA
Marjorie Howard, Tigard, OR
Miriam Huddleston, Portland, OR

Mrs. John W. Huff, Puyallup, WA
Mollie M. Hughes, Arlington, WA
Deb Jacobson, Mercer Island, WA
Grace Johnson, Bayview, WA
J. Yvonne Jones, Umpqua, OR
Mrs. Donald R. Jopp,
  Lakebay, WA
Kathleen Kahler, Camas, WA
M. Kappenthuler, Portland, OR
Charley Kidwell, Monte Rio, CA
Siegfried Kiemle, Seattle, WA
Celia Kircher, Dayton, OR
Ann Kosanovic-Brown,
  Seattle, WA
Virginia Lacy, Auburn, WA
Molly LaFayette
Mike Leadbetter, San Leandro, CA
Lena LeMoine, Lacey, WA
Mrs. Juanita Lewison-Snyder,
  Coos Bay, OR
Joanne Liantonio, La Conner, WA
Barbara M. Liggett,
  Snohomish, WA
Geraldeen Linnell,
  Vancouver, WA
Linda Lowber, Kent, WA
Steve Lower, Bear Wallow Farm,
  Mad River, CA
Stella Markee, Tillamook, OR
Sharon Marvin, Umpqua, OR
J.T. Mason, Anderson Island, WA
Evelyn McConnaughey,
  Eugene, OR
MaryAnn McDaniel, Port
  Angeles, WA
Kate McDermott, Port
  Angeles, WA
Dan and Joyce McGrath, Oregon
  City, OR
Michael McSwiggen,
  Portland, OR
George W. Mengelkoch,
  Portland, OR
Phyllis Michelson, Ridgefield, WA
Bev Miguel, Sebastopol, CA
Virginia Moore, Seattle, WA
Judy Moilanen, Port Angeles, WA
Lane Morgan, Sumas, WA
Jennifer Mueller, Willamina, OR
Virginia Naef, Deming, WA
Donna Nelson, Nelson Farms,
  Brownsville, OR
Mary Novotny, Eugene, OR
Torchy Oberg, Forest Grove, OR
Greg Oline, Rickrall, OR
Kate Olson, Banks, OR
Nora Olson, Lorane, OR
Mrs. John Owens, Port
  Angeles, WA
June Owens, Riddle, OR
Valerie Perry, Keizer, OR
Victoria Persons, Seattle, WA
Timothy R. Peterson, Port
  Orchard, WA

Liisa Prehn, Kirkland, WA
Carol Pryor, Cottage Grove, OR
Karen Pryor, North Bend, WA
Mary Rancourt, Eastsound, WA
Judy Rice, Middlesex, New York
Kathy Ringo, Seattle, WA
Caroline Robinson, Everett, WA
Mrs. F.W. Robinson, Port
  Angeles, WA
Myra Rose, Beaverton, OR
Garland Ross, Gold Hill, OR
Barbara Rozelle, Seattle, WA
Frank P. Ruemekorf, Bothell, WA
Mrs. Betty Ruiter
Pauline O. Sadler, Kirkland, WA
Hannah Salia, Seattle, WA
Dottie Schmiel, Lake Oswego, OR
Dorothy Schmitt, Chehalis, WA
John Separovich, Seattle, WA
Loretta Seppanen, Olympia, WA
Mrs. M. Shishido, Forest
  Grove, OR
Dorothy Simmons,
  Bremerton, WA
Paula Simmons, Sardis, BC
Joyce Smith, Vashon, WA
Janice Soderberg, Bellingham, WA
Bonnie Solonika, Sublimity, OR
Carolyn Stancik, Lynnwood, WA
Susan Stapoulos, Tacoma, WA
Kayla M. Starr, Cave
  Junction, OR
Mildred Stephenson, Half Moon
  Bay, CA
Debbie Stevens, Bonney Lake, WA
Ferne Supler, Edmonds, WA
Marilyn Tausend, Gig
  Harbor, WA
Pat Tennis, Bremerton, WA
E. Peter Terry, Tigard, OR
Sieglinde Thatcher, Corvallis, OR
Faye Treadaway, Deadwood, OR
Fay Trout, Memphis, TN
Phyllis Vallade, Seattle, WA
Bryan Vietmeier, Seattle, WA
Mary Vincent, Seattle, WA
Marshall A. Voight, Ferndale, WA
John L. Walsh, Navarro, CA
Lorretta Ward, Kotzebue, AK
Sherree Ward, Sequim, WA
John T. Waterman, Sutherlin, OR
Nina Wells, Independence, OR
Jan White, Tigard, OR
Joanne Polayes Wien, Seattle, WA
Benton G. Williams, Port
  Orchard, WA
Charles Williamson, Gig
  Harbor, WA
Pat Willis, Seattle, WA
Bárbara y Amando,
  Olympia, WA
Rhoda Yordy, Lebanon, OR
Hulda Zahler, Milwaukie, OR

Introduction

Beside my desk is a stack of old calendars scribbled with notations about my family's homestead. "Lots of cukes, first zucchini," reads the entry for August 8, 1981. "One gallon milk kicked over." (Our first years on these five acres taught us the literal meanings of many old sayings, and "Don't cry over spilled milk" was one of them.)

I keep these notes for reference, to remind myself that no matter how seductive the first warm week in April, it's still too early to set out tomatoes. But I value the evocations as much as the information. When the view from my window is of mud and bare branches, a flip through the pages of past summers brings back the promising smell of heated earth and the prickle of cucumber vines.

The contributed wisdom and experiences in this cookbook are satisfying in the same way. The following recipes, from gardeners throughout North America, celebrate the precious, scanty production of a first-year garden as well as the overwhelming harvests of a great year. Not only perfect new potatoes and peas, but frost-caught green tomatoes and bolting-to-seed kales are treated with ingenuity and respect. Thanks to these gardeners' tips, I have streamlined my tomato sauce technique and I finally know how to cook the cucumbers that always elude me until they have ballooned into grotesque yellow blimps.

As much as the food, I appreciate the glimpses into other gardens and kitchens. Through these recipes I can imagine feeding a family of eight on homegrown produce, or raising vegetables in Kotzebue, Alaska. I'm relieved to learn that I'm not the only one who has trouble growing onions, and I'm amazed at the culinary creativity inspired by the annual tidal wave of zucchini. The gardening kinship extends back through generations. I like to think of the grandmothers who passed on their recipes for Italian broccoli, Norwegian apple cake, Early American dill pickles, and more.

My own garden and kitchen have both been improved by this project. I want to thank all the contributors, and especially the ones who so promptly and graciously answered my queries.

Lane Morgan
Sumas, Washington
December 1990

Spring

Amelia's Shavé

Laura Hartmore
Snohomish, Washington

This recipe was told to me by my neighbor, Amelia Shostak, who moved here from the Soviet Union 10 years ago. This soup is also a childhood memory of my Jewish brother-in-law, whose relatives originated from Eastern Europe. It's very refreshing in hot weather.

1½ quarts water

1 bunch French sorrel (1 pound), cleaned and chopped

3 to 6 hard-cooked eggs, chopped

Chopped dill pickle to taste

3 green onions, chopped

1 cup sour cream or yogurt

Bring water to boil, add sorrel, and cook briefly. Cool; add eggs, pickle, green onions, and sour cream or yogurt. Serve cold.

Variation: Substitute young beets with greens for sorrel.

SERVES 6.

Don't cook sorrel in cast iron or aluminum cookware. It turns black.

Arugula and Potato-Leek Soup

....

Joyce Smith
Vashon, Washington

I altered this recipe to conform with the dietary requirements of low sodium, low fat.

3 tablespoons unsalted butter

2 medium onions, sliced

2 leeks, trimmed, halved lengthwise, washed well, and sliced

1 clove garlic, sliced

Salt

4 medium boiling potatoes (about 1½ pounds), peeled, quartered lengthwise, and sliced

2½ to 4 cups chicken or vegetable broth

⅛ teaspoon ground ginger

⅛ teaspoon nutmeg

⅓ cup cream or milk (I use 1 percent)

2 bunches coarsely chopped arugula leaves

Freshly ground black pepper

Melt butter in a saucepan. Add onions, leeks, garlic, and salt, tossing to coat. Cover and sweat vegetables, tossing occasionally, until softened, about 20 minutes. Add potatoes, broth, ginger, and nutmeg, stirring to combine. Raise heat, boil, skim off any froth. Simmer, partially covered, until potatoes are tender, 30 to 40 minutes. Remove from heat and purée or, if you like a chunkier soup, mash with potato masher. Add milk or cream and thin with additional broth if desired. (Soup can be prepared in advance to this point and then reheated at serving time.)

Return soup to boil, reduce heat, and scatter chopped arugula over surface. Cover and cook until wilted, about 2 minutes. Serve with freshly ground black pepper to taste.

SERVES 6.

Asparagus Soup

· ·

Pat Tennis
Bremerton, Washington

4 cups water

4 bouillon cubes, any flavor

1 large onion, chopped

1 large green pepper, chopped

Lots of chopped asparagus

Flour

Margarine

Salt and pepper

Bring water to a boil. Add bouillon, onion, green pepper, and asparagus and cook until tender. Put in blender. For each blenderful, add 2 tablespoons flour, 1 tablespoon margarine, salt, and pepper to taste. Blend and serve.

Variations: Asparagus may be substituted with—you choose—tomatoes, leeks, peas, carrots, zucchini, broccoli, etc.

SERVES 6.

Most catalogs will tell you to buy leek seeds every year. Don't believe it. Germination is excellent the second year and pretty good the third.

Kale Blossom Soup

· ·

Loretta Seppanen
Olympia, Washington

A favorite spring recipe (make at tax time).

STOCK

2 tablespoons olive oil

1 carrot, chopped

1 celery stalk, chopped (or dried
  leaves of celeriac or lovage)

Handful of kale stems, rough cut

Lower ends of asparagus (optional)

4 parsley branches, chopped

1 lovage branch, chopped

1 bay leaf

8 cups cold water

SOUP

3 tablespoons olive oil

1 medium potato, sliced

1 handful kale blossoms, just before
  they bloom, chopped

3 shallots, sliced

1 leek, white part only, sliced

2 or 3 handfuls kale leaves and
  stems, chopped

8 branches parsley and chervil,
  chopped (leaves only)

1 handful sorrel, chopped

1 bunch chard or spinach, chopped

7 cups stock (recipe below)

Nutmeg

Champagne vinegar

Yogurt

To make the stock, sauté vegetables and herbs in olive oil for 5 minutes. Add water and bring to a boil. Simmer 20 to 25 minutes, remove from heat, and strain. (Stock can be made ahead and refrigerated for 4 or 5 days or frozen.)

When stock is ready, sauté potatoes and kale blossoms in olive oil. Add 1 cup stock. Cover and stew 15 minutes. Add remaining greens and herbs. Cover and cook until wilted, about 5 minutes. Add remaining stock and bring to a boil. Simmer 10 minutes. Remove from heat and cool briefly. Purée solids. Slowly add liquids. Return to soup pot and keep warm.

Serve with dollop of yogurt, nutmeg, and a little vinegar.

SERVES 6 TO 8.

Spinach Salad

··

Jane Becklake
Saltspring Island, British Columbia

¼ cup oil

¼ cup vinegar

¼ cup sugar

½ teaspoon dried rosemary
   (more if fresh)

½ teaspoon salt

Radishes

Onions

Nectarine or peach (optional)

Spinach

Make a marinade of the oil, vinegar, sugar, rosemary, and salt. Slice radishes and onions into rings (if you can afford it, throw in some sliced nectarines or peaches) and soak in marinade for as long as possible. Clean and tear spinach into bite-sized pieces. Drain off marinade (it can be reused if kept in refrigerator) and add radishes and onions to spinach. Toss and serve.

Edible Pea Pods

··

Marjorie Howard
Tigard, Oregon

Pick the peas—and eat them—in the garden. I have raised them for many years but have never brought one into the kitchen.

———— ❦ ————

Peas, like corn, should be picked just before eating as sugar conversion to starch begins rapidly after picking.

Jersey Potatoes

. . . .

E. Peter Terry
Tigard, Oregon

As with the delight of many Oregon gardeners picking the first ears of sweet corn, so is this pleasure matched, or even surpassed, by the joy of harvesting the first of the Jersey-type new potatoes in England.

Boiled with fresh mint and served buttered they are an absolute delight.

Main Dish Swiss Chard

. . . .

Deanne Adams
Vancouver, Washington

3 tablespoons oil

1 to 2 pounds Swiss chard (6 cups coarsely shredded leaves and 1 cup diced stems; separate leaves and stems)

3 tablespoons whole wheat flour

½ envelope nonfat dry milk, reconstituted in 1 cup water

1 tablespoon instant chicken broth granules

1½ teaspoons Worcestershire sauce

¼ teaspoon hot-pepper sauce

½ cup shredded Swiss cheese (optional)

2 hard-cooked eggs (optional)

Paprika

In a large heavy-bottomed kettle, heat oil and add diced chard stems. Sauté until crisp-tender. Add flour and stir to make a roux. Add reconstituted milk, chicken broth granules, and Worcestershire and hot-pepper sauces. Cook over low heat until thickened. Add chard leaves and stir to coat with sauce. Reduce heat to barely simmer and cook until chard is tender, stirring occasionally. Swiss cheese may be added just before stirring or the chard may be transferred to a serving dish and topped with sliced eggs. Garnish with paprika.

SERVES 3 OR 4.

New Potatoes Vinaigrette

Victoria Persons
Seattle, Washington

12 to 16 (5 pounds) small new
   potatoes

Vinaigrette (recipe below)

1 cup chopped green onion,
   including some tops

2 tablespoons chopped parsley

1 tablespoon chopped chives

Salt and pepper

VINAIGRETTE

½ cup olive oil

3 tablespoons tarragon or basil
   vinegar

1 teaspoon prepared mustard

3 teaspoons honey

Steam or boil potatoes until just tender. If skins are tough, peel; otherwise leave peels on and just slice. Put vinaigrette ingredients in shaker jar, shake well, and pour over potatoes. Toss with green onion, parsley, chives, and salt and pepper to taste. Serve warm or cold.

SERVES 4 TO 6.

Wireworms are the enemy of the garden-stored potato, burrowing past the skin and leaving the tuber vulnerable to rot. That's one reason you should bring potatoes in for storage. But you can use potato pieces as wireworm traps. Put a piece of potato in the ground, mark the spot, and dig it up to discard along with the worms.

Spinach Parmesan

Karen Pryor
North Bend, Washington

A rich party dish.

3 pounds fresh spinach

2½ tablespoons butter

½ cup whipping cream

½ teaspoon nutmeg

6 tablespoons grated Parmesan cheese

1 tablespoon minced fresh chives or
green onions

More Parmesan

Clean spinach, remove stems, and steam 10 minutes. Drain, cool slightly, and chop coarsely. Add butter, cream, and nutmeg and mix well. Put mixture in covered casserole and microwave 4 minutes, stirring twice (or bake in a conventional oven 20 minutes at 350°F, stirring once). Add Parmesan and chives or green onions and mix again.

At this point you can hold the dish several hours or overnight in the refrigerator. Before dinner, sprinkle with more Parmesan and bake 15 minutes in a preheated 400°F oven, uncovered, just until hot and bubbly.

SERVES 6 (OR 4 GREEDY
SPINACH LOVERS).

*Winter spinach will do better if sown
on a ridge of soil for better drainage.*

Stuffed Chicken Breasts

··

Mary Novotny
Eugene, Oregon

6 boneless, skinless chicken breasts

2 bunches spinach

2 tablespoons butter

Garlic powder

Feta cheese

1 egg, beaten

2 cups dry, seasoned bread crumbs

2 tablespoons vegetable oil

GRAVY

2 tablespoons butter

1 cup sliced mushrooms

2 tablespoons flour

1 cup white wine

1 cup chicken stock

1 tablespoon lemon juice

Preheat oven to 350°F. Pound chicken breasts. Steam spinach, drain, and toss with butter and garlic powder to taste. When spinach mixture is cool, lay it on individual chicken breasts and sprinkle with feta. Roll chicken around filling and fasten with toothpick. Dip in egg and then roll in bread crumbs. Brown in oil in frying pan and then transfer to baking pan and bake, covered with foil, for 45 minutes.

Meanwhile, make the gravy. Melt butter in saucepan. Add mushrooms and sauté. Add flour and cook until browned. Add wine, chicken stock, and lemon juice. Simmer to thicken. Remove chicken to a platter, pour sauce over, and serve.

SERVES 6.

Stuffed Morel Mushrooms

Virginia Naef
Deming, Washington

1 pound medium to large firm-
  fleshed morels

SAUCE

4 tablespoons butter

1 or 2 medium cloves fresh garlic,
  minced

FILLING

1½ cups cooked white or long-grain
  brown rice

½ cup cooked wild rice

¼ to ½ cup finely chopped chives or
  green onions

½ cup leftover cooked, flaked fish or
  smoked salmon (optional)

½ teaspoon coarse ground black
  pepper (optional)

Preheat oven to 350°F. Briefly soak morels in a briny salt solution to help eliminate insects. Drain. Remove stalks and save if desired for sauces and stews.

Melt butter and stir in garlic for sauce.

Combine all filling ingredients. Gently stuff the mushrooms with filling and place mushrooms filling-side-up in a shallow 2-quart baking dish or casserole. Drizzle with sauce and bake until well heated, 30 to 45 minutes.

Editor's Note: The morel species common to the Northwest is the early morel, *Verpa bohemica.* It appears on damp ground under cottonwoods, just as the trees are starting to leaf out. The timing and place are important, especially for novice gatherers, because somewhat similar-looking poisonous species can be found in the late summer and fall, and in the spring under conifers rather than cottonwoods. Some people are allergic to morels, so sample them with discretion.

SERVES 2 TO 4.

Sunday Morning Eggs

....

John L. Walsh
Navarro, California

After my heart attack I reduced my egg input from 14 a week down to two a week. As a result, those two eggs had to satisfy my longing for eggs for a full seven days! This recipe comes closest to doing so.

1 tablespoon olive oil

4 fresh eggs at room temperature

1 egg substitute (equivalent to
   2 eggs)

2 tablespoons dry vermouth

⅛ teaspoon pepper

2 tablespoons fresh chopped chives

Warm the olive oil in the cooking skillet. A cast iron skillet is preferred. Whisk remaining ingredients until mixed but not frothy. Pour into the warmed skillet and cook over low heat. As the eggs firm up around the edges, pull them into the center so the liquid portion flows out to the edge. When the whole mass is firm but still moist, remove from the burner so the warmth of the skillet completes the cooking. With a spoon, chop and stir until the mixture loses its moist look and serve immediately on two warmed breakfast plates.

Variation: For larger groups, the eggs may be stretched by mixing in ½ cup of torn bread for every 8 eggs. The cooking should be slowed by adding a little water or nonfat milk to the mixture.

SERVES 2.

Turkey Stir-Fry

· ·

Margot Becker
Snohomish, Washington

This stir-fry evolved the first year we had a vegetable garden. We never got enough of any one vegetable for a meal, so I made stir-fry.

1 clove garlic, minced

3 tablespoons soy sauce or tamari

½ cup chicken broth

½ cup white wine

½ pound turkey breast, sliced thin

Spray shortening

Ginger, minced

Dashes of sesame oil

*Vegetables to taste, but be sure to
    have some from each category:*

*onions—yellow, leeks, or shallots (be
    generous with the milder onions)*

*cole—broccoli or cauliflower in
    small florets; kohlrabi, sliced*

*leafy—pac choi, spinach or Swiss
    chard, Chinese or regular cabbage*

1 carrot, sliced diagonally

*1 or more stalks celery, sliced
    diagonally*

Mushrooms, sliced (optional)

Snow peas, cut in half

Green or red peppers, diced

1 teaspoon cornstarch

1 tomato, cut in eighths

Mix garlic, soy sauce, broth, and wine. Add turkey and marinate. Heat spray shortening, a few dashes of sesame oil, and ginger in wok. Drain turkey, reserving marinade. Add turkey to wok, toss and cook over high heat until done, 2 to 3 minutes. Remove from pan.

Spray shortening again and add dashes of sesame oil. Add vegetables, starting with those that need more cooking (onions, carrots, broccoli, cauliflower, celery) and ending with greens, mushrooms, and snow peas. Toss and cook until not quite done. Return meat to pan and mix.

Mix cornstarch into marinade and pour over. Toss and stir until sauce bubbles and thickens. Vegetables should still be crunchy. Garnish with sliced tomato. Serve with rice or Chinese noodles and more soy sauce.

Variations: Blanched green beans and cucumbers (cooked briefly) are good. Also water chestnuts (when garden is more bare).

SERVES 3 OR 4.

Zubriak

Kate McDermott
Port Angeles, Washington

2 pounds small curd cottage cheese or ricotta

2 eggs

1 tablespoon chopped fresh parsley

Salt and pepper

½ cup melted butter

Garlic powder

1 pound chopped fresh spinach, cooked, drained, and squeezed (or use your blanched and frozen supply)

1 package (12 ounces) lasagne noodles

4 cups (1 pound) grated Monterey jack cheese

1 cup grated Parmesan cheese

Preheat oven to 350°F. Mix together cottage cheese, eggs, parsley, salt, pepper, and butter. Add garlic powder to spinach. Cook lasagne in boiling water. Grease 12-by-15-inch pan and layer in this order: noodles, cottage cheese mix, Monterey jack, Parmesan, spinach. Repeat layers again. Bake 30 minutes.

SERVES 8.

Fresh Strawberry Pie

· ·

Mildred Stephenson
Half Moon Bay, California

¾ cup sugar

3½ tablespoons cornstarch

1 cup cold water

3 tablespoons white corn syrup

1 tablespoon lemon juice

½ tablespoon butter

3 tablespoons strawberry-flavored
dry gelatin

1 basket (or more) hulled
strawberries

Prebaked pastry for 9-inch pie

Mix together sugar, cornstarch, water, and corn syrup in order given. Bring to boil, lower heat, and then cook, stirring, until mixture is thick and clear. Remove from stove and add lemon juice, butter, and gelatin. Stir well. Cool. Add strawberries, mixing carefully. Pour into pie shell and chill. Serve with whipped cream.

SERVES 8.

The sweet soil that makes most of your garden happy is bad for strawberries. Covering the strawberry beds with fir boughs for the winter will lessen the compacting effect of winter rains and acidify the soil at the same time.

Rhubarb Cream Pie

Alice Bond
Lyons, Oregon

1½ cups sugar

3 heaping tablespoons flour

2½ cups stewed rhubarb

3 egg yolks, slightly beaten

⅓ cup orange juice

Grated rind of 1 orange

1 tablespoon butter

Prebaked pastry for 9- or
    10-inch pie

Mix sugar and flour together. Add to rhubarb and cook slowly until thickened, stirring constantly. Stir into egg yolks, return to heat, and cook 1 minute longer. Remove from heat, add orange juice, rind, and butter. Cool. Pour into pie shell, top with meringue, and brown.

Editor's Note: Here's a suitable meringue recipe, provided by Donna Dreessen of Port Orchard, Washington: Beat 2 egg whites and ¼ teaspoon cream of tartar until stiff but not dry. Beat in gradually ½ teaspoon vanilla and 4 tablespoons sugar. Spoon onto pie and bake 12 to 15 minutes at 350°F.

MAKES ONE 9- OR 10-INCH PIE.

Rhubarb can be picked for the first time the year after planting. Pick only two weeks that year. Later the harvest can go on for about six weeks. Pick no more than two-thirds of the stalks of any one plant at a time. Allow the young stalks to continue to grow. Throw away the leaves. You can get early, blanched rhubarb by covering plants with big pots just when they start to come up in the spring.

Fresh Green Goddess/ Garden Herb Dressing

Joanne Polayes Wien
Seattle, Washington

This is my standard summertime salad dressing. I don't actually measure any of the ingredients, but it always comes out great. If it comes out too tart, add some mayonnaise. Dressing thickens when stored in the refrigerator.

1 bunch fresh chives (a good-sized handful)

A combination of fresh herbs (tarragon, oregano, savory, thyme)—several sprigs of any or all of the above, leaves only

1 cup yogurt

2 tablespoons olive oil

1 or 2 tablespoons lemon juice or vinegar

Purée in a blender or food processor and refrigerate. Keeps one week or more.

MAKES ABOUT 1¼ CUPS.

Lettuces like cool weather, but they are prone to rot during the rainy season. Plant them far enough apart so that air can circulate between the plants. Remove the bottom leaves if they are limp or touching the ground. Growing winter lettuce is easier if you stick with relatively compact, upright varieties like Winter Density. A ring of sand or wood ash below the plant will also help thwart the soilborne fungi.

Harmony Farm Garlic Butter

Carol Danz
Harmony Farm, Cave Junction, Oregon

½ pound butter, softened

3 or more cloves garlic, minced

2 tablespoons fresh chopped parsley

2 tablespoons fresh chopped celery
leaves

2 tablespoons fresh or frozen chopped
sweet basil

1 teaspoon celery seed

2 tablespoons fresh chopped chives

1 teaspoon summer savory

1 teaspoon oregano

¼ cup grated Parmesan cheese
(optional)

Mix all ingredients and stir occasionally until butter has set. Chill. For lower cholesterol, make a "better butter" substituting safflower, olive, corn, or canola oil for half the butter.

MAKES APPROXIMATELY
½ POUND.

Chile Salsa

··

Timothy R. Peterson
Port Orchard, Washington

For dipping with tortilla chips or adding to your favorite Mexican recipes.

4 fresh jalapeño peppers, minced

1 clove garlic, crushed

1 small bunch fresh cilantro

1 teaspoon crushed black pepper

*3 green onions, chopped, including
    green tops*

4 ripe tomatoes, diced

Pinch oregano

¼ cup tomato sauce

¼ cup water

Salt and pepper

Combine jalapeños, garlic, cilantro, black pepper, onions, tomatoes, and oregano. Add water and tomato sauce until mixture reaches proper consistency. Add salt and additional pepper to taste.

MAKES ABOUT 2 CUPS.

Low-Cal Dressing for Raw Veggies

Molly LaFayette

1 cup nonfat plain yogurt

1 cup Miracle Whip Light

1 clove garlic, grated

½ to 1 teaspoon no-salt seasoning or salt

1 packet sugar substitute or 1 teaspoon turbinado sugar

Mix all ingredients well. If using raw sugar, let sit for 5 minutes and then mix again. Can be stored two weeks in refrigerator. For a richer-tasting dressing, use regular Miracle Whip and regular yogurt. (No-salt seasoning, yogurt, and turbinado sugar can be bought in some supermarkets and most health food stores.)

Good dip veggies are celery, green peppers, radishes, green onions, carrots, broccoli, mushrooms, and cauliflower. We put tomato wedges on the platter, too. Arrange bite-sized pieces according to contrasting colors for a prettier-looking dish.

MAKES 2 CUPS.

Quick Cucumbers

Debbie Arney
Olympia, Washington

I guess this isn't really a recipe—just a suggestion. Sprinkle seasoned rice vinegar (sushi vinegar) over sliced cucumbers and serve. We use it on chunks of tomato, cucumber, and onions also. We never have any leftovers.

No-Salt Seasoning

···

Siegfried Kiemle
Seattle, Washington

5 teaspoons onion powder

1 tablespoon garlic powder

1 tablespoon paprika

1 tablespoon dry mustard

1 tablespoon thyme

½ teaspoon white pepper

½ teaspoon celery seed

Combine and store in a tightly covered container.

MAKES ¼ CUP.

Poppy Seed Dressing

···

Charley Kidwell
Monte Rio, California

¼ cup honey

¼ cup apple cider vinegar

2 tablespoons S&S Hot Mustard
  (Page 29)

2 tablespoons poppy seeds

4 tablespoons grated onion

4 teaspoons salt (optional)

¾ cup oil

Combine all ingredients except oil and mix well. Stir in oil a little at a time.

S&S Hot Mustard

Charley Kidwell
Monte Rio, California

½ cup honey

¼ cup vinegar

1 egg

4 tablespoons dry mustard

2 tablespoons grated fresh horseradish
  or 3 tablespoons prepared
  horseradish or 2 teaspoons fresh
  mashed garlic and 2 teaspoons
  chili powder

Combine all and cook in double boiler until thick.

MAKES ABOUT 1 CUP.

Lemon-Yogurt Dressing

Diana Anderson
Enumclaw, Washington

1 cup plain low-fat or non-fat yogurt

3 tablespoons reduced calorie
  mayonnaise

2 tablespoons lemon juice

1 tablespoon plus 1 teaspoon Dijon
  mustard

⅛ teaspoon garlic powder

⅛ teaspoon pepper

Combine all ingredients and serve with fresh leaf lettuce, Healthy Salad (Page 118), or other mixed vegetables.

MAKES ABOUT 1¼ CUPS.

Spiced Butter or Margarine

....

Margaret Hedin
Port Angeles, Washington

2 cups butter or margarine

1 medium onion, peeled and
    chopped

2 tablespoons chopped garlic

1 tablespoon chopped ginger

¼ teaspoon basil

¼ teaspoon fine cardamom

¼ teaspoon oregano

Melt butter or margarine over low heat in 2-quart skillet, stirring gently. Increase heat slowly and bring to a boil. When covered with foam, stir in remaining ingredients. Reduce heat to very low and simmer undisturbed for 45 minutes. Slowly strain through a fine sieve. Pour into a jar, cover tightly, and store in refrigerator or at room temperature. It will solidify when cold. Use as needed. Will keep two or three months.

P. S. Use strained seasonings on minced turkey or chicken.

MAKES ABOUT 2 CUPS.

Sweet/Sour Salad Dressing

Sieglinde Thatcher
Corvallis, Oregon

This tastes super, especially if you have lived in Germany. Mutti added dill weed to it to pour over sliced cucumbers.

⅓ cup fresh or bottled lemon juice

*2 tablespoons honey or 3 envelopes
sugar substitute*

¼ to ½ teaspoon salt

2 cups safflower oil

Combine lemon juice, honey or sugar substitute, and salt in glass measuring cup. Heat in microwave for a moment to dissolve salt. Add oil (I use expeller-pressed oil) and beat with small beater or fork until thickened.

MAKES 2½ CUPS.

Tarragon Vinaigrette

Mary Novotny
Eugene, Oregon

¾ cup oil

5 tablespoons white wine vinegar

2 tablespoons lemon juice

2 teaspoons sugar

½ teaspoon salt

*4 teaspoons chopped fresh tarragon or
2 teaspoons dried and crumbled*

Mix and refrigerate before using. Wonderful on fresh garden lettuce.
Variation: Omit tarragon and add fresh raspberries for a delightful summer salad dressing.

MAKES ABOUT 1 CUP.

Tofu Salad Dressing/ Dipping Sauce

Sky Groth
Emeryville, California

The kitchen is a place of process. Proportions vary with the occasion.

Tofu

Fresh grated ginger

Chopped garlic

A little cilantro is nice

*Vinegar (rice, cider, or wine),
2 tablespoons per pound of tofu*

Sesame oil

Soy sauce

*A little honey or sugar (to bind
flavors)*

Grated onion

A little hot sauce

I have a food processor, which easily blends this up, but it can be done by hand. Add cold broth or vegetable stock if sauce is too thick. Milk, buttermilk, or even yogurt also has worked.

Editor's Note: You could use seasoned rice vinegar (sushi vinegar) and omit the honey or sugar.

Zesty Italian Salad Dressing

Margot Becker
Snohomish, Washington

1 cup salad oil or olive oil

1 cup wine vinegar or cider vinegar

1 cup fresh or reconstituted lemon
   juice

Half a large onion, chopped

2 large cloves garlic, minced

1 tablespoon fresh oregano or
   1 teaspoon dried

1 tablespoon fresh basil or 1 teaspoon
   dried

3 tablespoons fresh parsley or 1 tablespoon dried

Half a dried red chile pepper

Sprinkle of coarse-ground black
   pepper

Shake of Worcestershire sauce

½ cup grated Parmesan cheese

1 small can anchovies or at least
   1 tablespoon anchovy paste

1 tablespoon dried parsley or 3 tablespoons fresh

Place all ingredients in blender and
blend well. (Fresh herbs are really
best; they will make the dressing
rather green.) Note: Ingredients
can be varied as to quantity. The
traditional recipes all call for ⅔ oil
to ⅓ vinegar, but I prefer the
above. You can use a dash of water
to cut the sharp vinegar taste.
Some people also like a pinch of
sugar in this dressing.

Serve with a salad of mixed garden greens, cucumbers or zucchini,
radishes, tomatoes, green onions,
or leeks.

MAKES ABOUT 1 QUART.

---

*It takes 300 pounds of water to grow
a pound of lettuce.*

Creamy Cumin Dip

....

Joan Hogan
Albany, Oregon

1 pint cottage cheese

½ teaspoon ground cumin

*4 green onions, sliced, green tops
and all*

Mix cottage cheese in blender if you want it smooth. Stir in cumin and onions and it's ready, although it gets better with an hour or two to meld the flavors. Great with corn chips or crudités.

MAKES 1 PINT.

Flavored Butters

....

J.P. Frances
Mustang, Oklahoma

1. To each 1 tablespoon of butter add 2 or 3 drops hot-pepper sauce and chopped parsley.

2. Add chopped chives to butter.

3. To each tablespoon olive oil or melted butter add ½ teaspoon cider vinegar and chopped parsley, dill weed, or cilantro.

4. Garlic butter: Peel 1 to 3 cloves garlic and then crush. Pound in mortar with ¼ cup butter. Use on steak, vegetables, or garlic bread.

5. Into each tablespoon softened butter, mix 1 teaspoon bacon bits, either real or artificial.

Leftover flavored butters should be kept up to three weeks in freezer rather than merely refrigerated.

Summer

Cilantro Soup

Marilyn Tausend
Gig Harbor, Washington

This is an adaptation of a wonderful Mexican soup given to me by a friend, Maria Dolores Izabál of Mexico City.

4 medium zucchini, cooked in salted
   water

6 cups chicken stock

1 cup cilantro, packed

4 tablespoons butter

Half a medium onion, chopped fine

2 tablespoons cornstarch, dissolved in
   cool broth

2 jalapeño chiles

¼ pound feta cheese, cubed

Diced jalapeño chiles to taste

3 tortillas, cut into strips and lightly
   fried

Blend zucchini thoroughly with the chicken stock in blender or food processor. Add cilantro and blend again.

Melt butter in soup pot and sauté onion until transparent. Add cornstarch mixture, zucchini purée, whole chiles, and salt, if necessary. Simmer 10 minutes.

Serve in bowls and pass around fried tortilla strips, diced chiles, and cheese.

Editor's Note: Marilyn Tausend is co-author of *Mexico the Beautiful Cookbook.*

SERVES 6.

Cool High-Protein Summer Soup

....

Sieglinde Thatcher
Corvallis, Oregon

They say that necessity is the mother of invention. Well, pain can be partner to it. Having a temporary crown, I had to forgo my usual salad as could not chew. Loving my first-year garden's produce, the idea hit me t throw the whole shebang into the blender. The result? A wonderful summe soup. I tested the soup on my 23-year-old daughter, who loved it but coul not believe how it was made.

½ cup water

⅓ to ½ cup Sweet/Sour Salad Dressing (Page 31)

1 stem parsley (yes, the stem, too!)

1 handful of lettuce (no Iceberg!), about 3 large leaves

1 medium tomato

½ zucchini (about 3 inches)

½ cucumber

2 boiled fertilized eggs, peeled (if you want the calcium, leave the peel on, but it spoils the soup)

⅛ teaspoon salt

1 can (4 ounces) tiny shrimp, drained, or 1 can (6½ ounces) undrained tuna

Pour everything into blender, cover, and liquefy. Add more water if needed. Pour into large bowl if you want a complete meal, or pour into two smaller ones and share with a friend. Tastes better yet if chilled first.

SERVES 1 OR 2.

Gazpacho

....

Sarah Davis
Portland, Oregon

1 clove garlic, minced

4 or 5 fresh tomatoes, peeled and
   chopped

1 cucumber, peeled and diced

1 medium yellow onion, minced

1 bell pepper, diced

2 cups tomato juice

⅓ cup olive oil

⅓ cup red wine vinegar

Salt and pepper to taste

Mash garlic in a large bowl. Mix together with tomatoes, cucumber, onion, bell pepper, tomato juice, oil, and vinegar. Add salt and pepper. Chill soup until very cold. Serve.

SERVES 4 TO 6.

Setting out the warm weather plants is always a touchy business in northern gardens. If you wait too long they get leggy and potbound, but if you put them out in the cold they will sit and sulk for weeks, if they survive at all. If you must transplant in a dreary, drizzly June, water in the roots with warm water, and continue to use warm water until the young plants start growing.

Mediterranean Minestrone

....

Kathleen Kahler
Camas, Washington

2 pounds beef soup bones

3 pounds beef, sliced

4 quarts water

—or—

2 quarts cooked soup meat

2 quarts soup broth

2 quarts water

_____

1 quart tomato juice

1 pint tomato sauce

2 medium onions, quartered

¼ cup chopped parsley

2 teaspoons basil leaves, crushed

½ teaspoon ground black pepper

¼ teaspoon garlic powder

2 bay leaves

1½ cups soaked dry beans

2 cups sliced carrots

2 cups sliced celery

4 cups uncooked shell macaroni

1 pint green beans

1 cup green peas

Bring meat and broth or water to boil. Add tomato juice, tomato sauce, onions, herbs and spices, and soaked dry beans. Return to boil and simmer 1½ hours. Add carrots and celery and simmer 30 minutes longer. Heat to a boil, and add macaroni, green beans, and peas. Simmer 15 to 20 minutes.

MAKES 7 QUARTS.

Quick-Fresh Minestrone

Linda Lowber
Kent, Washington

2½ quarts chicken stock

8 mushrooms, sliced

1 can garbanzo beans (8¾ ounces), drained

1 small can (8 ounces) stewed tomatoes

1 large tomato, chopped

1 jar artichoke hearts (6 ounces), undrained

3 carrots, sliced

1 onion, chopped

1 clove garlic, chopped

1 small zucchini, sliced

1 large celery heart with leaves, chopped

¼ cup chopped parsley

1 small bunch spinach, stems removed

1 cup broken vermicelli

Salt and freshly ground pepper

Freshly grated Parmesan cheese

Pour chicken stock in large pot. Add all vegetables except for spinach. Cover and cook over medium heat until celery and carrots are crisp-tender, about 30 minutes. Add spinach and vermicelli and cook another 10 minutes. Season with salt and pepper. Ladle into bowls, top with Parmesan, and serve immediately. Also good with pesto added in the last 10-minute cooking period.

SERVES 8.

Sweet Fruit Soup

Margaret Hedin
Port Angeles, Washington

2 cups unsweetened applesauce

½ cup pitted prunes

½ cup raisins

1 cup sugar

½ cup tapioca flour or cornstarch

1 heaping teaspoon cinnamon

1 cup pitted pie cherries

1 medium orange, peeled and sliced
(optional)

1 medium lemon, peeled and sliced
(optional)

2 cups grape or blackberry juice

Heat applesauce. Add prunes and raisins and simmer, covered, for 10 minutes. Mix together sugar, tapioca flour or cornstarch, cinnamon, and cherries and stir into applesauce mixture. Add orange and lemon (if used). Simmer, covered, 15 minutes or until mixture is slightly thickened. Stir in grape or blackberry juice. Remove from heat and chill.

SERVES 10.

Peat moss, if you can afford it, makes a better mulch than sawdust because it doesn't rob the soil of nitrogen. The mulch saves watering and weeding, keeps soil temperature more even, and helps discourage slugs. It also helps keep rotting fruit from contaminating the soil.

Easy Bulghur Salad

· ·

Bonnie Solonika
Sublimity, Oregon

1 cup bulghur wheat, soaked 1 hour
  in 1 cup warm water

2 or 3 tomatoes, chopped

1 cucumber, peeled and chopped

1 stalk celery, chopped

1 carrot, chopped

Olives and onions, chopped, to taste

¼ cup lemon juice

2 tablespoons olive oil or vegetable oil

2 or 3 tablespoons chopped parsley

1 teaspoon salt

1 teaspoon pepper

Add tomatoes, cucumber, celery, carrot, and olives and onions (if used) to bulghur. Mix together lemon juice, oil, parsley, salt, and pepper. Pour over bulghur mixture and refrigerate a few hours before serving.

SERVES 3 OR 4.

Fresh Green Bean Salad with Basil and Tomatoes

Nikki Anderson
Wauna, Washinton

This makes a great luncheon salad.

2 pounds (8 cups) tender young green beans

1 pint cherry tomatoes

½ cup thinly sliced red onion (use green onion if reds aren't ready)

1 bunch (about 4 ounces) fresh basil

1 cup mayonnaise

Salt and pepper to taste

2 tablespoons toasted chopped almonds (optional)

More basil leaves for garnish (optional)

Remove stem ends from beans and string if necessary. Blanch beans in heavily salted water (to retain green color) until "al dente." Rinse in cold water (to stop cooking and remove most salt) and set aside to drain.

Remove basil leaves and discard stems and blossoms. Wash and dry leaves and chop very fine. Slice onions and quarter tomatoes, and toss with beans, basil, and mayonnaise in large bowl. Adjust seasoning with salt and freshly cracked pepper.

Garnish with fresh basil leaves or toasted chopped almonds.

SERVES 6 TO 8 AS A SIDE DISH.

Marinated Vegetable Salad

Barbara Rozelle

½ cup julienned carrots

¾ cup diagonally sliced celery

1 cup green beans in 1-inch slices

2 cups broccoli florets

2 cups cauliflower florets

1 can black olives, drained

¼ cup sliced green pepper (optional)

1 cup Italian salad dressing

Cook carrots and celery separately until barely tender. Drain. Cook green beans until tender. Blanch broccoli and cauliflower separately by pouring boiling water over and bringing to boil for one minute. Cover and let stand 5 minutes and then drain. Toss vegetables, olives, and green pepper (if used) in large bowl. Heat salad dressing and pour over. Chill before serving. Keeps for several weeks.

SERVES 4 TO 6.

Pasta Salad with Pesto

· ·

Victoria Persons
Seattle, Washington

1 pound pasta (shells, spirals, or
tortellini)

1 pound cucumbers

Salt

2 chopped tomatoes or 15 cherry
tomatoes

4 green onions, chopped

½ pound broccoli (about 6 cups),
blanched

4 tablespoons chopped parsley

4 tablespoons chopped basil

2 tablespoons olive oil

2 cloves garlic

¼ cup Parmesan cheese

Cook pasta, drain, and set aside.
Peel cucumbers and slice ¼-inch
thick. Toss with salt and let sit.
Meanwhile, chop tomatoes and
onions; separate broccoli into small
florets. Drain cucumbers. Put parsley, basil, olive oil, garlic, and
cheese in blender. Mix until
smooth. Toss all vegetables and
pasta together in bowl. Pour on
sauce from blender and toss again.

SERVES 6 TO 8.

Spicy Chunky Veggie Salad

Kate Olson
Banks, Oregon

Tomatoes, cucumbers, green peppers, celery, and onions, all chopped into 1-inch pieces

Carrots, sliced ¼-inch thick (optional)

Avocados, radishes, and Jerusalem artichokes, chopped (all optional)

Salt

Paprika

Cayenne or chili powder

Juice of ½ lime or ¼ lemon per serving

Place chopped vegetables in a bowl, whatever amount seems appropriate. Add salt, paprika, and cayenne or chili powder to taste. Add lime juice or lemon juice and a little water. Stir briskly and serve. Different, delicious, and a meal in itself.

Jerusalem artichokes will grow more than 10 feet tall in good soil, which is too high for their shallow roots in a windy climate. Cut them back when they get over 5 feet and they will do just fine, blooming off the side shoots that grow when the main branch is cut.

Chinese-Style Pork with String Beans

....

Mrs. M. Shishido
Forest Grove, Oregon

2 tablespoons oil

1 clove garlic, crushed

1 slice ginger, crushed

½ pound pork, sliced thin and flat

1 teaspoon salt

1 tablespoon soy sauce

1 pound string beans, cut in 1-inch
   lengths

1 small carrot, cut 1 inch long by ¼
   inch wide

¾ cup water or stock

1 tablespoon cornstarch mixed in 1
   tablespoon water

Seasoning

Heat pan with oil. Slightly brown ginger and garlic. Add pork and fry 1 minute. Mix salt and soy sauce together, add to pork mixture, and cook for another minute over low flame. Add string beans, carrots, and water. Cook a few minutes without cover until vegetables are tender. Thicken slightly with cornstarch mixture.

SERVES 4 OR 5.

—————— ——————

Never pick beans in the rain. Damaging fungi can be transferred from one plant to another on your damp hands. In general, keep the foliage dry by watering only the roots. But if your beans are in bloom during a long dry spell, you should spray the blossoms lightly with lukewarm water.

Colorful Summertime Pasta

Dottie Schmiel
Lake Oswego, Oregon

This recipe is a bit time-consuming, but easy and will reap compliments for the cook!

12 ounces pasta (fusilli or a small shell variety)

1 tablespoon olive oil

2 large tomatoes, diced

¾ cup julienned fresh basil leaves

1 pound ricotta cheese

½ cup plain yogurt

¾ cup freshly grated Parmesan cheese

4 or 5 cloves garlic, minced

½ teaspoon freshly ground black pepper

4 or 5 cups assorted chopped vegetables (some suggestions: gold zucchini, broccoli, peas, carrots, green beans, cauliflower)

⅓ cup chopped filberts

1 tablespoon butter

1 red bell pepper, sliced for garnish

Fresh parsley

Nasturtium flowers

Boil pasta, drain in colander, toss with olive oil, and set aside. Combine tomatoes and basil in bowl; set aside. Place ricotta, yogurt, Parmesan, garlic, and pepper in a large skillet and simmer 20 minutes.

Meanwhile, prepare and steam assorted vegetables until crisp-tender, about 3 to 5 minutes. Sauté filberts in butter until golden.

Place pasta on a very large serving platter, making a well in the center. Spoon vegetables into well. Top pasta (and some of the vegetables) with cheese sauce. Spoon tomato-basil mixture over all; top with filberts. Garnish with red pepper, parsley, and nasturtiums.

Serve with French or Tuscan bread.

SERVES 6 FOR DINNER.

Burger Garden in a Skillet

·····································

Diana Anderson
Enumclaw, Washington

1 pound hamburger

1 medium onion, chopped

⅛ teaspoon pepper

1 teaspoon poultry seasoning

½ teaspoon paprika

1 medium carrot, shredded

1 cup corn

1 cup cut green beans

1 cup fresh mushrooms

1 small can tomato sauce

½ cup water

Brown beef and onion. Drain. Mix in remaining ingredients and cook slowly, covered, until vegetables are tender. Good over rice.

SERVES 4.

Different Okra

·····································

Carl Hanscam
Occidental, California

⅓ cup chopped bacon

Half or whole medium onion, chopped

Tender whole okra, under 2 inches long

Salt and pepper

Oregano (optional)

Tomatoes, sliced thick

2 to 4 heaping tablespoons cornmeal (the difference)

Fry bacon and drain off all but 2 tablespoons fat. Remove bacon and sauté onion until transparent. Add okra and stir until warm. Season with salt, pepper, and oregano (if used). Return bacon to pan and mix. Cover with sliced tomatoes. Sprinkle cornmeal on top, cover, and steam approximately 30 minutes.

SERVES 2 TO 4.

Cauliflower and Pea Curry

···

Jan Cole
Pittsburg, California

1 medium head cauliflower, cut into
   florets

2 medium potatoes, scrubbed and
   cubed

2 tablespoons butter

1 medium onion, chopped

1½ tablespoons poppy seeds

1½ tablespoons curry powder

1½ teaspoons fresh grated ginger

1 teaspoon cumin seed

¼ teaspoon hot-pepper flakes

2 cups unflavored yogurt

1 tablespoon cornstarch

2 cups fresh shelled peas or sugar
   snaps, cut in small pieces

Steam cauliflower and potato until just crisp-tender, 8 to 10 minutes. Drain. Meanwhile, melt butter in large Dutch oven over medium heat. Add onion and sauté until transparent and soft. Add poppy seeds, curry powder, ginger, cumin, and hot-pepper flakes. Stir for 1 minute. Mix yogurt with corn-starch, and then stir it into curry mixture. Add cauliflower, potatoes, and peas and heat until all vege-tables are heated through but still crisp-tender. Serve with whole wheat chapatis or pita bread for scooping up every bit of this spicy curry!

SERVES 4 TO 6.

——————— ———————

Rabbits are my biggest problem in growing peas. The most efficient way I have found to deal with them is to plant the peas along two long rows of chicken wire, and then close off the ends with more chicken wire, making a long, rectangular fence with the peas inside. Once the peas are big enough to make it on their own I re-move the ends for easier weeding. An old-time way to protect pea seeds from mice is to put holly clippings in the trench at planting time.

Corn Fritters

· ·

Jan White
Tigard, Oregon

2 cups corn

½ cup milk

½ cup flour

1 teaspoon baking powder

1 teaspoon melted butter

2 eggs

1 teaspoon salt

Pepper

Mix all of above and fry in hot oil.
Serve with butter.

SERVES 4.

Corn Pudding

· ·

Virginia Moore
Seattle, Washington

2 eggs

1 cup milk

*2 cups fresh corn kernels or drained
canned corn*

½ teaspoon salt

⅛ teaspoon pepper

*1½ tablespoons melted margarine or
butter*

½ cup finely chopped green pepper

½ cup grated cheese (optional)

Preheat oven to 325°F. Beat eggs.
Add milk, corn, salt and pepper,
margarine or butter, and green
pepper. Mix well and pour into
well-greased casserole. Sprinkle
with cheese (if used). Bake 45 minutes or until silver knife comes out
clean.

SERVES 6.

Corn with Peppers

Deanne Adams
Vancouver, Washington

1 teaspoon olive oil

1 teaspoon cumin seed

1 each red and green bell pepper, fresh or frozen, cut in 1-inch pieces

¾ cup sliced sweet white onion

3 cups fresh or frozen whole kernel corn

½ teaspoon sea salt (optional)

Heat cumin seed in olive oil over low heat 5 minutes. Add sliced onion, increase heat to medium, and cook another 5 minutes. Add peppers and corn. Mix well, cover, and cook until corn is tender and pepper is crisp-tender.

SERVES 4.

Butter-Steamed Corn

Barbara M. Liggett
Snohomish, Washington

2 tablespoons butter

4 cups fresh or thawed corn kernels

4 tablespoons water

Salt

Melt butter in a wide skillet on high heat. Add corn and water. Cover and cook, stirring frequently, for 4 minutes (3 minutes for frozen corn). Salt to taste.

SERVES 4 OR 5.

Eggplant Casserole

· ·

Jan White
Tigard, Oregon

Flour

1 or 2 eggs, beaten

1 cup crushed bread crumbs

1 large eggplant, cut in thin rounds

⅓ cup plus 1 teaspoon vegetable oil

½ pound mushrooms

2 small green onions, chopped

1 cup shredded Cheddar cheese

Place flour, eggs, and bread crumbs in separate bowls. Dip eggplant slices first in the flour, then the eggs, then the crumbs. Fry in ⅓ cup oil until browned and soft in the middle. Drain on paper towels as you sauté onions and mushrooms in remaining teaspoon of oil.

Preheat oven to 350°F. Layer eggplant, mushroom mixture, and cheese in a casserole, ending with sprinkling of cheese. Bake 20 minutes.

SERVES 4.

Eggplant Tomato Casserole

J. Yvonne Jones
Umpqua, Oregon

*1 large or several small eggplant
(about 1½ pounds), chilled*

2 eggs, beaten

1½ teaspoons salt

Pepper

2 tablespoons melted butter

2 or 3 tablespoons chopped onion

½ teaspoon oregano

½ cup dry bread crumbs

2 large tomatoes, sliced thin

½ cup grated Cheddar cheese

Paprika

Preheat oven to 375°F. Slice eggplant. Steam or simmer about 10 minutes, and then mash into a large bowl. Add eggs, salt, butter, pepper, onion, oregano, and bread crumbs.

Butter a shallow 1½-quart baking dish. Cover bottom with half the tomatoes. Spoon eggplant mixture over tomatoes and spread evenly. Arrange rest of tomatoes over eggplant and sprinkle cheese over the top. Sprinkle with paprika and bake for 45 minutes. For variation, add garlic or green pepper.

SERVES 6.

Focaccia

....

Audrey Edmonds
Poulsbo, Washington

Editor's Note: Focaccia is a northern Italian specialty. It starts with a flat bread, thicker and softer than pizza crust. In its simplest form, the dough is simply brushed with olive oil, sprinkled with salt, and baked until browned. It is eaten warm as a snack or light meal. More substantial toppings call for precooked garden vegetables. The plainer the topping, the more important it is to use a good quality dough.

DOUGH

1 package (1 tablespoon) active dry yeast

1½ cups warm water

½ teaspoon salt

2 tablespoons olive oil

3½ cups flour (all or part may be whole wheat)

Vegetable topping

Salt and pepper

—or—

1 loaf frozen bread dough

To make focaccia dough, sprinkle yeast over water in large bowl. Let stand 5 minutes to soften. Stir in salt and olive oil. Add 2½ cups flour and stir to blend. Beat with a mixer or by hand until dough is elastic and stretchy, 3 to 5 minutes. Stir in remaining flour. Knead until dough is smooth and springy. Place in an oiled bowl. Turn dough over to oil top. Cover bowl with plastic wrap. Let rise until doubled, about 45 minutes in a warm place or in the refrigerator until the next day. Knead on a lightly floured board to expel air. (If using frozen bread dough, follow package directions for thawing and initial rising times.)

Coat bottom of a 10-by-15-inch baking pan with 1 tablespoon olive oil. Place dough in pan. Press and stretch dough to fill pan evenly. Cover pan lightly with plastic wrap and let rise in warm place until doubled again, 45 to 60 minutes. Drizzle 1 tablespoon oil over dough. With your fingers, push dough into pan corners and gently press down all over, forming dimples in the surface. Cover dough with one of the toppings and sprinkle lightly with salt and pepper. Bake at 400°F until dough is well browned on edges and bottom, 35 to 45 minutes. Can hold up to 8 hours at room temperature and can be reheated, covered, in a 350°F oven.

EGGPLANT-PEPPER TOPPING

1 large red bell pepper, seeded and coarsely chopped

2 medium eggplants (about 2 pounds total), in ¾-inch cubes

3 tablespoons olive oil

2 cups shredded mozzarella cheese

2 tablespoons chopped parsley

Preheat oven to 450° F. Mix pepper and eggplants with oil and bake until eggplant begins to soften and lightly brown, 20-25 minutes. Sprinkle cheese over focaccia dough. Scatter eggplant mixture over cheese and bake according to focaccia dough directions. After baking, sprinkle with parsley.

POTATO TOPPING

3 large potatoes (about 2 pounds), peeled and sliced thin

¼ cup olive oil

1 tablespoon fresh or dry rosemary leaves

¼ teaspoon pepper

In a 10-by-15-inch baking pan, mix potatoes, olive oil, rosemary, and pepper. Bake in a 400°F oven until potatoes begin to turn translucent and light gold, 15 to 20 minutes. Cool about 5 minutes, then gently loosen potatoes from pan with a wide spatula and carefully separate slices. Arrange evenly over dimpled dough and bake.

AUDREY EDMONDS'S TOPPING

2 green peppers, sliced

2 large yellow onions, sliced

2 zucchini, sliced

Grated Cheddar cheese to taste

Sauté vegetables in a little oil until crisp-tender. Spread on dough, sprinkle with cheese, and bake. I'm sure other garden things could be used: yellow crookneck squash, tomatoes in season, perhaps even cauliflower or broccoli—along with herbs especially liked by the individual.

SERVES 12.

Fragrant Indian Vegetables

Barbara M. Liggett
Snohomish, Washington

½ pounds eggplant, sliced about ¼
inch thick

4 tablespoons vegetable oil, divided,
plus a little for brushing

1 large new potato (about ¾
pound), scrubbed but not peeled

2 medium onions (1 pound), coarsely
chopped

2 large cloves garlic, minced

1½ teaspoons ground cumin

1 bay leaf

1 head cauliflower, florets cut into
bite-sized pieces

1½ tablespoons coarsely grated fresh
ginger

6 canned Italian plum tomatoes,
well drained

½ cup chopped cilantro

1 cup or more nonfat plain yogurt

Heat oven broiler and cover broiler
pan with aluminum foil. Arrange
eggplant slices on broiler pan and
brush lightly on both sides with
oil. Broil slices as close to heat as
possible, watching that the slices
do not burn. When one side is
brown, turn and brown on second
side. Total broiling time is about
15 minutes.

Cut potato slices into quarters
and sauté in 2 tablespoons of oil
until slices begin to brown and
soften. Remove and set slices aside.
In same skillet pour remaining oil
and sauté onion and garlic in oil
for a minute or two. Add cumin
and bay leaf and mix well. Continue to sauté until onions soften
and begin to color. Add cauliflower,
ginger, and tomatoes, breaking up
tomatoes with your hands before
adding them to pan. Cover and
cook about 5 minutes, until
cauliflower is done.

When eggplant is cool enough
to be handled, trim off skin, cut
into large chunks, and add to skillet to heat through. Serve with
cilantro and yogurt.

Editor's Note: Fresh-picked
Japanese eggplant varieties like
Short Tom will cook much faster
than the big European types.

SERVES 3 OR 4.

French Fry Bake

M. Kappenthuler
Portland, Oregon

⅓ cup butter

1¼ cups chopped green pepper, divided

¾ cup chopped celery

⅓ cup flour

½ teaspoon salt

⅛ teaspoon pepper

3 cups milk

¾ cup shredded American cheese

¾ cup shredded carrot

¾ cup corn

⅓ cup chopped pimiento

32 ounces frozen French-fried potatoes

Preheat oven to 375°F. In large saucepan, cook ¾ cup green pepper and celery in butter until tender but not brown. Stir in flour, salt, and pepper. Add milk at once. Cook, stirring, until mixture is bubbly and then continue cooking one minute more. Add half the cheese, carrots, corn, and pimiento, stirring until cheese is melted. Put the potatoes in a 9-by-13-inch baking dish, cover with cheese sauce, and bake 30 minutes. Sprinkle remaining cheese atop and bake 5 minutes more. Garnish with additional green pepper.

SERVES 12.

Garden Leftover Gumbo

Mrs. Juanita Lewison-Snyder
Coos Bay, Oregon

Created in 1989 as a way to help get rid of extra vegetables grown in our garden. We still manage to overplant each year.

½ cup butter or margarine

1 medium onion, sliced into rings and separated

1 cup sliced mushrooms

1 stalk celery, sliced thin

1 carrot, sliced thin

1 medium zucchini, cubed

1 medium crookneck squash, cubed

2 medium potatoes, cubed

1 cup sugar snap peas, pods and all, sliced in thirds

1 cup frozen corn kernels

1 handful broccoli florets

1 handful cauliflower florets

2 tomatoes, cut into wedges

1 small can olives, sliced thin

1 small can kidney beans, drained

Salt and pepper

1 pound ground beef, cooked and drained

Melt butter or margarine in large skillet. Sauté onion first, and then add mushrooms and celery. Gradually add carrots, zucchini, squash, potatoes, corn, peas, broccoli, cauliflower, tomatoes, olives, and kidney beans. Add salt and pepper to taste. Add ground beef, cover, and turn down heat to barely simmer. Let heat through for about 10 minutes.

Serve hot with bread and butter or biscuits. Delicious!

SERVES 4.

Good for You Spaghetti Sauce

Margot Becker
Snohomish, Washington.

Spray shortening

1 large onion, chopped

3 cloves garlic, chopped

1 stalk celery, chopped

Half a green pepper, chopped

1 cup grated carrot

1 cup grated zucchini

*1 cup fresh mushrooms or 3 table-
spoons dried*

*1 pound ground turkey and/or turkey
sausage*

1 cup tomato paste

2 cups tomato sauce

*1 medium can whole tomatoes or
1½ cups reconstituted dried
tomatoes*

2 tablespoons chopped fresh parsley

2 tablespoons chopped fresh basil

2 tablespoons chopped fresh oregano

1 tablespoon fennel or anise seeds

2 bay leaves

Hot red pepper flakes

Dash of black pepper and salt

1 cup dry red wine (optional)

Pasta

Parmesan cheese

Sauté onion, garlic, celery, pepper, carrot, zucchini, and fresh mushrooms with vegetable shortening spray. Add meat and brown. There shouldn't be any fat; if there is, press it out in a sieve. Add fresh or reconstituted mushrooms and tomatoes. (Add soaking water too if you are using dried tomatoes.)

Add wine (if used) and season to taste with herbs and spices. Simmer 2½ hours if using fresh home-made tomato paste and sauce and home-dried tomatoes. With commercially canned tomatoes, 1 hour simmer is enough. Taste and adjust seasonings. Serve over freshly cooked pasta or baked spaghetti squash and sprinkle with Parmesan. I also use same sauce for lasagne.

SERVES 6.

Green Beans Marinara

Victoria Persons
Seattle, Washington

4 cups (1 pound) snapped or French cut green beans

¼ cup olive oil

4 teaspoons garlic vinegar or tarragon vinegar

1 clove garlic, chopped fine

2 teaspoons honey or sugar

1 tomato, chopped

¼ cup bread crumbs

¼ cup grated Romano or Parmesan cheese

Preheat oven to 350°F. Steam beans until just tender. Rinse in cold water to stop cooking. Combine next four ingredients in a jar, cover tightly, and shake well. Mix beans and tomatoes in casserole. Cover with sauce and sprinkle with bread crumbs and cheese. Bake 15 to 20 minutes.

SERVES 4 TO 6.

Giannangelo Farms Pesto Sauce

Vicky Giannangelo
Friday Harbor, Washington

3 cloves garlic

4 tablespoons roasted sunflower seeds

½ cup olive oil

2 cups fresh basil

½ cup grated Parmesan cheese

Put garlic, sunflower seeds, and olive oil in blender and purée. Add basil and reblend. Stir in cheese.

MAKES ABOUT 1 CUP.

Green Beans with Sour Cream and Almonds

....

Deanne Adams
Vancouver, Washington

1 teaspoon cold-pressed oil

½ cup coarsely chopped sweet white onion

3 or 4 cups fresh, frozen, or canned green beans

¾ cup sour cream at room temperature

½ teaspoon sea salt or ¾ teaspoon herb salt or herb salt substitute

Freshly ground coarse black pepper

½ cup coarsely chopped toasted almonds

Sauté onion in oil until crisp-tender. Add green beans (and 1 tablespoon water if fresh beans are used). Steam quickly until bright green and crisp-tender. Drain. Add sour cream and seasonings and mix well. Reheat, covered, over very low heat. Transfer to serving bowl and top with toasted almonds.

Variation: Sauté bacon, Canadian bacon, or lean ham. Discard fat. Reserve meat. Add onion to pan and sauté until crisp-tender. Follow recipe above, topping with crisp sautéed meat instead of almonds.

SERVES 4.

Pesto Suggestions

....

Suzy Cook
Bainbridge Island, Washington

Pesto freezes very well. It tastes like a burst of summer sunshine in the dead of winter. It also is good baked in the center of a long loaf of homemade whole wheat bread. Pecans are a good substitute for the traditional pine nuts.

Homegrown Marinara

· ·

Frank P. Ruemekorf
Bothell, Washington

I have a recipe for a basic marinara sauce that is simple, versatile, healthy, and very tasty. It contains no salt, no cholesterol, very little fat, and all the ingredients, except the olive oil, can be raised in the home garden, although canned tomato paste (check ingredients list for salt content) is a convenient and healthy substitution for tomato pulp.

2 tablespoons olive oil

1 medium onion, peeled and diced

2 or 3 cloves garlic, finely minced or crushed

1 can (6 ounces) tomato paste and 3 cans water or 4 cups peeled, seeded, diced Roma-type tomatoes, cooked until they collapse

2 tablespoons fresh sweet basil or 1 tablespoon dried

1 tablespoon fresh oregano or 1½ teaspoons dried

3 whole, dried red chiles

Sauté onion in olive oil over medium heat until onion is transparent. Add garlic and sauté a moment longer to soften the flavor of the garlic. Add tomato paste and water (or cooked tomato pulp) and stir until mixed thoroughly. Add basil, oregano, and chiles. When sauce starts to bubble, reduce heat and simmer for 20 to 30 minutes, stirring occasionally. Remove chiles and discard. (Be sure to use the chiles. When whole, so the seeds don't escape, they add no discernible heat even for the most sensitive palate, and they add a wealth of flavor to the sauce.)

This sauce is excellent as-is on any pasta, rice, steamed vegetables such as cauliflower, or in lasagne. For added color, texture, flavor, and nutrition, add a cup or so of your favorite in-season garden vegetable such as chopped spinach, grated zucchini, broccoli florets, or grated carrot during the last 5 minutes of cooking.

No-Cook Puttanesca

Deanne Adams
Vancouver, Washington

3 anchovies, chopped

⅓ cup chopped parsley

1 pound plum tomatoes, fresh or
    frozen, seeded and sliced very thin

2 cloves garlic, pressed or chopped
    fine

⅓ cup sliced black olives

1½ tablespoons capers

2 tablespoons olive oil

¾ teaspoon hot-pepper flakes

Salt and pepper to taste

½ pound rotelle pasta

Parmesan cheese (optional)

Combine in order the anchovies, parsley, and tomatoes. Add garlic, olives, capers, olive oil, hot-pepper flakes, salt, and pepper and mix gently.

Cook pasta in lightly salted boiling water. Drain and add to sauce. Mix well.

Note: In winter I warm the sauce slightly in the microwave before adding pasta.

SERVES 4.

Nori Spaghetti Sauce or Pizza Topping

Evelyn McConnaughey
Eugene, Oregon

Nori is the common Japanese name for our seaweed called *Porphyra*. It grows abundantly on rocks in the upper intertidal area of the seashore. Dried nori may be substituted. I have made this recipe using my own garden fresh tomatoes and fresh basil.

2½ cups fresh nori, firmly packed, or ¼ cup dried nori (available in Asian markets and natural foods stores)

2 tablespoons oil

2 cups mushrooms, sliced

2 cups sliced onions

5 cloves (⅓ cup) elephant garlic, grated

1 quart chopped, peeled tomatoes

1 small zucchini (½ cup), sliced or chopped

¼ cup chopped green and jalapeño peppers

1½ teaspoons each chopped fresh basil, oregano, thyme, and marjoram

1 tablespoon chopped parsley

Salt and pepper to taste

2 tablespoons white wine

Grind nori in meat grinder or sauté and then crush. Combine all ingredients in a saucepan and cook until thickened. For spaghetti sauce, you may add tomato sauce, more white wine, and Parmesan cheese. Serve over pasta or parboiled *Gracilaria* (*ogo*), a spaghetti-shaped reddish seaweed popular in Hawaii and Asia. For pizza topping, add enough tomato paste to get a spreadable sauce. Spread onto a rolled, unbaked crust on greased pizza tin. Top with grated mozzarella or Monterey jack cheese and *Nereocystis* dill pickles (recipe below). Bake at 400°F until crust is brown, about 15 minutes.

MAKES ABOUT 1 QUART.

Curried Yellow Crookneck

J.T. Mason
Anderson Island, Washington

2 tablespoons butter

1 medium onion, sliced thin

4 or 5 medium squash (2 to 2 ½ pounds), sliced ½-inch thick

3 tablespoons hot water

½ teaspoon salt

¼ teaspoon ground black pepper

¼ teaspoon sugar

Curry powder to taste

⅔ cup yogurt

In a large sauté pan, melt butter over low heat. Add onion and cook until onion is glazed but not brown. Add squash, hot water, salt, and pepper. Bring to boil, then cover. Cook for 5 minutes longer. Add sugar and curry powder and cook, uncovered, 10 minutes over medium heat. Stir frequently. Add yogurt and heat through without boiling. Serve immediately.

SERVES 4.

A lot of old homes and homesteads have stands of comfrey. You can't easily get rid of it so you might as well put it to use. The leaves are high in potash and make an excellent mulch for potatoes and beans, and the pink and blue flowers are favored by bees. If you are making your first comfrey tea, be sure you know the difference between comfrey and foxglove. The young plants look similar, and foxglove tea can kill you.

Microwave Summer Squash

Robert Brown
Hillsboro, Oregon

2 tablespoons butter or margarine

1 onion, chopped

1 clove garlic, pressed

2 quarter-inch slices summer

   sausage, cubed (optional)

3 small crookneck squash or

   zucchini, in 1-inch cubes

2 tablespoons grated Parmesan cheese

Melt butter or margarine in 2-quart microwave dish. Stir in onion, garlic, and sausage (if used). Cook 3 or 4 minutes on high. Add squash, stir to coat, and cook another 2 or 3 minutes on high until crisp-tender. Sprinkle on cheese and mix. Let sit 5 minutes before serving.

SERVES 4.

My Dutch Vegetables

Grace Johnson
Bayview, Washington

1 cucumber, peeled and chopped

1 medium onion, chopped

1½ teaspoons apple cider vinegar

1 shake fines herbes mixture

Mayonnaise

Salt and pepper to taste

Mix cucumber, onion, vinegar, and fines herbes. Add mayonnaise, salt, and pepper to taste. Very tasty with meat and/or fish.

MAKES ABOUT 1½ CUPS.

Nereocystis Dill Pickles

Evelyn McConnaughey
Eugene, Oregon

2 quarts hollow bulbs and stipes
(stems) of Nereocystis, cut in ½-
inch pieces

2 cups sugar

1 tablespoon celery seed

1 tablespoon turmeric

1 tablespoon mustard seed

1 tablespoon pickling spices

1 medium onion, sliced

1 teaspoon salt

1 clove garlic or ¼ teaspoon powdered garlic

1½ cups white vinegar

Combine all ingredients and let stand 3 hours. Heat to boiling and seal in hot jars. Needs no further processing. This is a very easy method, and gives an excellent product.

Editor's Note: This recipe is from McConnaughey's booklet, *Sea Vegetable Recipes from the Oregon Coast*, published in 1980 and distributed by the Oregon Institute of Marine Biology. The booklet is "dedicated to Nature and society's relation to it—an almost lost world of self-reliance, individuality, home-grown flavors in a food market dominated by artificiality, uniformity and multinational profits." *Nereocystis* is the Latin name for the common bull kelp. When gathering for the kitchen, don't use the old ones tossed up on the beach.

MAKES ABOUT 3 PINTS.

Patty Pan Squash with Dill and Turmeric

....

Deanne Adams
Vancouver, Washington

6 three-inch diameter patty pan
squash

1 tablespoon chopped young dill head

½ to ¾ teaspoon turmeric

Sea salt or herb salt (optional)

1 teaspoon butter or cold-pressed oil
(optional)

Section each squash into 6 wedges. Sprinkle with dill and turmeric. Add 1 tablespoon water. Steam until just tender. Serve with optional ingredients if desired, but the squash is delicious without them.

SERVES 4.

Broiled Tomatoes

....

Mike Leadbetter
San Leandro, California

We always used to have this with fresh salmon, steamed potatoes, and a green salad. Out of the garden, of course.

1 tomato

¼ to ½ teaspoon butter

Basil, fresh or dried

Minced garlic and Parmesan cheese
(both optional)

Core tomato and cut in half horizontally. Top with butter and sprinkle with basil, garlic, and Parmesan (if used). Put a little butter on top. Put under broiler (approximately 4 inches away) for 3 to 5 minutes or until hot through and slightly brown on top.

1 SERVING.

Pizza without a Crust

Miriam Huddleston
Portland, Oregon

I learned this from an old Italian farmer in Kansas. It is a great way to use the bits and pieces of veggies that don't quite fit the serving dish.

2 tablespoons olive oil

3 or 4 cups bite-sized cut mixed vegetables (I like broccoli, flat beans, onion, green pepper, and cauliflower)

2 cloves garlic, diced

1 teaspoon oregano

½ teaspoon black pepper

Salt, pepper, and hot-pepper sauce to taste

3 eggs, beaten

½ cup shredded Cheddar cheese

¼ cup grated Parmesan cheese

½ cup shredded mozzarella cheese

Preheat oven to 375°F. In a heavy skillet, sauté vegetables and garlic in oil until half cooked. Stir in oregano, salt, pepper, hot-pepper sauce, and eggs. Cook gently until eggs are nearly set. Top with cheeses and bake 10 minutes or until cheese is melted.

SERVES 4.

Sunflowers should be harvested when about half the yellow ray flowers have fallen from the heads. Cut heads with a foot or so of stem still attached and hang them upside-down in a dry area with good air circulation until they have dried. Tie a piece of cheesecloth around each head if you need to keep the seeds from falling.

Hulled seeds can be frozen or canned. To hull, drop seeds in boiling water for a short time or crack with pliers or a nutcracker.

Ratatouille (Rat-Tat-Tooey)
French vegetable stew

· ·

Mrs. John Owens
Port Angeles, Washington

3 tablespoons olive oil

2 cups chopped onion

2 cloves garlic, minced

8 cups unpeeled diced eggplant

4 cups diced zucchini

1 cup diced green pepper

4 cups diced ripe tomatoes

1 teaspoon dried basil

1 teaspoon dried oregano

1 teaspoon dried thyme

1 teaspoon dried marjoram

1 tablespoon to 1 cup tomato paste

Salt and pepper to taste

1 cup grated cheese (Cheddar,
Parmesan, or provolone) for
garnish

In large pot, heat olive oil and
sauté onion and garlic until
translucent but not brown. Add
eggplant and cook over medium
heat for about 5 minutes, stirring
often. Add remaining vegetables
and herbs. Cook 15 minutes more.
Add tomato paste and a little water
if needed. Season with salt and pepper. Cook 5 minutes more. Serve
or freeze for later use. This can be
doubled or tripled with ease.

SERVES 8 TO 10.

Ideas for Ratatouille

Mrs. John Owens
Port Angeles, Washington

These are from an old garden paper.

Use as a pasta sauce. Add extra Italian tomato sauce and/or meatballs if desired.

Put cold or hot ratatouille in pocket sandwiches with cheese and sprouts.

Spoon over baked potatoes.

Serve over cooked rice, with a poached egg on top and a dollop of hollandaise sauce.

Stuff into hollowed-out tomatoes, blanched green peppers, hollowed-out eggplant halves (prebaked 20 minutes), or parboiled winter squash. Sprinkle with grated Parmesan cheese. Bake at 350°F until hot.

Add diced cooked meats and serve over pasta or rice.

No-Fat Ratatouille

....

Myra Rose
Beaverton, Oregon

This is a delicious, low-calorie casserole that improves when reheated to serve a second day.

2 large onions, peeled

4 to 6 tender, 6-inch-long summer squash

4 large ripe tomatoes

1 medium eggplant, sliced (optional)

1 large sweet pepper

4 cloves elephant garlic, sliced

Salt and pepper

Bottled barbecue sauce

¼ cup water

Parmesan cheese

Slice vegetables ¼-inch thick. Place in layers in a 10-inch skillet, starting with onions. Sprinkle each layer lightly with salt, more heavily with pepper, 1 teaspoon barbecue sauce, and some sliced garlic. Alternate vegetables as you layer them in.

Add water, cover, and cook over moderate heat until natural juices of vegetables begin to flow. Simmer, covered, for 30 minutes or until vegetables are tender. Adjust seasonings. Serve hot or at room temperature, sprinkled with Parmesan.

SERVES 3 OR 4.

Marian Brown's Eggplant Casserole

Lane Morgan
Sumas, Washington

6 cups peeled and cubed eggplant or
   summer squash

2 onions, chopped

Bacon fat

⅔ cup dry cracker crumbs

2 tablespoons melted butter

2 small tomatoes, chopped

1 egg, beaten

Salt and pepper

Paprika

1 tablespoon butter

Salt eggplant or squash, let sit 15 minutes, and then steam about 15 minutes or until tender. Drain and let cool before mashing. You should have about 4 cups mashed.

Preheat oven to 350°F. Sauté onions in bacon fat. Add tomatoes and cook down. Remove from heat and add mashed eggplant or zucchini, melted butter, and ½ cup cracker crumbs. Fold egg in gently and add salt and pepper to taste. Bake, uncovered, in shallow casserole for 1 hour. Sprinkle with remaining crumbs and paprika and dot with butter for last 10 minutes of cooking.

SERVES 6.

Tomato blossom drop can be minimized simply by tapping the plant to distribute pollen.

Barbecued Vegetables

Lane Morgan
Sumas, Washington

Eggplants

Summer squash

Peppers, from sweet to medium hot

Sweet onion

Balsamic vinegar or red wine vinegar and a little brown sugar

Oil

Soy sauce

Salt and pepper

Basil, chopped

Oregano, chopped

Hot-pepper sauce (optional)

Slice vegetables lengthwise. Make them wide enough so they won't fall through your grill. Make marinade using equal proportions oil and vinegar and remaining ingredients to taste. Pour over vegetables, mix, and let stand at room temperature at least an hour, preferably more. Drain vegetables and cook on the barbecue until really done. Your goal is a toasted-marshmallow effect—brown to almost black on the outside, melting soft within. Sprinkle with a little more salt and serve. Remaining marinade can be saved for salads, new potatoes, or steamed vegetables.

SERVES A CROWD.

Sautéed Summer Squash with Tomatoes and Herbs

Bryan Vietmeier
Seattle, Washington

1½ tablespoons good olive oil

1 tablespoon chopped shallots or thinly sliced sweet onion

1 tablespoon chopped garlic

1 medium zucchini, sliced ¼-inch thick

2 medium yellow patty or crookneck squash, sliced ¼-inch thick

1 tablespoon fresh chopped herbs: thyme, parsley, basil, rosemary, oregano

2 medium ripe tomatoes, diced (paste variety best)

¼ cup white wine

2 tablespoons butter (optional)

Salt and pepper to taste

Romano or Parmesan cheese, grated (optional)

In large skillet, sauté shallot and garlic in oil until transparent. Add squash and herbs and cook until just tender. Stir occasionally and use a lid if needed. Add tomatoes and heat through. Splash with white wine, add butter (for richness and flavor), and lightly sprinkle with cheese, if desired.

SERVES 4.

Stuffed Garden Vegetables

Donna Dreessen
Port Orchard, Washington

2 medium green peppers, tops removed and center seeded

2 medium red peppers, tops removed and center seeded

2 medium purple onions, tops removed and center hollowed

2 medium white potatoes, peeled and center hollowed

2 large zucchini, center hollowed

2 medium eggplants, halved and center hollowed

½ cup butter

FILLING

1¾ pounds lean ground beef, lightly sautéed

¼ pound ground pork, lightly sautéed

½ cup bread crumbs

½ cup onion, chopped

2 cloves garlic, minced or garlic powder

2 tablespoons parsley, minced

1 teaspoon seasoned salt

½ teaspoon cumin

1 tablespoon lemon juice

1 egg, beaten

½ cup white wine

½ teaspoon nutmeg

½ teaspoon white pepper

SAUCE

2 tablespoons butter

1 clove garlic, minced

3 tablespoons flour

1 can (10 ounces) chicken broth

⅔ cup white wine

1 tablespoon lemon juice

1 tablespoon minced parsley

1½ cups peas and diced carrots, cooked

⅓ cup chopped onion

Melt butter in large skillet. Sauté each vegetable for 5 minutes and remove from heat. (Vegetables used may vary according to taste and availability.) Combine filling ingredients and toss lightly. Fill each vegetable and place in large baking dish. (Hard varieties of potatoes may be baked 15 or 20 minutes before stuffing.) To make sauce, sauté onion and garlic in butter until transparent. Blend in flour to make a roux. Slowly add chicken broth and wine, stirring constantly, until completely dissolved. Add lemon juice, parsley, and peas and carrots. Cook over low heat 3 minutes or until mixture thickens. Pour sauce over stuffed vegetables, cover, and bake 25 to 30 minutes.

SERVES 6.

Scalloped Sweet Onions

J. Yvonne Jones
Umpqua, Oregon

3 large or 6 medium sweet onions, sliced thin

5 tablespoons butter, divided

3 tablespoons flour

1 teaspoon salt

Pepper

1½ cups milk

1 cup diced celery

½ cup pecan halves

Parmesan cheese

2 tablespoons sherry

Preheat oven to 350°F. Sauté onions in 3 tablespoons of the butter in large skillet. Remove onions and add remaining 2 tablespoons butter. Blend in flour, salt, and pepper. Gradually add milk and cook over low heat until thick and smooth, stirring constantly. Add sherry and stir to blend. Cook celery briefly in small amount of water in microwave or on stovetop, until barely tender. Drain. Layer onions, celery, and sauce in buttered baking dish. Sprinkle pecans over top. Sprinkle Parmesan over all and bake until hot and bubbly, 20 to 30 minutes.

SERVES 6.

Stuffed Squash Blossoms

Lane Morgan
Sumas, Washington

Squash blossoms are strongest early in the day, before the sun's heat makes them go limp. Pick them in the morning and refrigerate until stuffing time. Meat or seafood mixtures also are used for stuffing, but I like this version best. You can substitute cheeses to suit your taste, but at least one should be strongly flavored or the dish will be too bland.

½ cup beer

½ cup flour

1 egg

Hot-pepper sauce

½ cup grated mozzarella or Monterey jack cheese

¼ cup crumbled Gorgonzola or blue cheese

¼ cup grated Parmesan cheese

1 tablespoon butter

2 teaspoons chopped Italian parsley

12 squash flowers (these are fragile so it's wise to pick a few extra)

1½ cups oil for frying

Salt and pepper

Mix together the beer, flour, and egg. Add salt and hot-pepper sauce to taste. Let this batter rest at least 15 minutes. Meanwhile, combine cheeses, butter, and parsley and work into a paste by hand or in a blender or food processor. Open the flowers gently and remove the stamen and pistils. Put a dab of filling into each flower and twist the top of the petals to seal the package. Heat oil in a saucepan. Dip each flower in batter and place gently into hot oil. Cook no more than 3 at a time until golden brown, about 2 minutes. Remove with a slotted spoon and drain on paper towels. Sprinkle with salt and pepper and serve warm.

SERVES 4 TO 6.

Stuffed Sunburst Squash

....

Loretta Seppanen
Olympia, Washington

A favorite summer recipe.

6 sunburst squash

⅓ cup yogurt cheese (drain yogurt for
  at least 12 hours; use the liquid
  on house plants)

2 tablespoons grated cheese (Parmesan is great)

1 tablespoon pine nuts

⅓ cup fine bread crumbs (whole
  wheat or oat bran)

2 sprigs lemon thyme (use just the
  leaves)

2 small basil leaves

1 green onion

Preheat oven to 400°F. Microwave whole squash with a little water, 8 to 10 minutes on high, 5 to 8 minutes sitting, until tender (or steam until tender). Drain. When squash are cool enough to handle, cut off tops and save. Remove and save seeds and pulp, leaving a ⅛-inch shell.

Purée seeds and pulp in blender or food processor. Add remaining ingredients and stuff shells with mixture. Dish can be made ahead to this point. Replace squash tops and put squash in an ovenproof pan with a small amount of water. Bake 10 minutes and serve hot. You can eat the shell as well as the stuffing.

SERVES 6.

Stir-Fry Eggplant and Zucchini

John Separovich
Seattle, Washington

1 small eggplant, peeled and cut in ½-inch cubes

¼ cup (or more) corn oil or olive oil

1 medium onion, chopped

Garlic to taste, chopped

1 medium zucchini

2 medium tomatoes or 10 cherry tomatoes, sliced or halved

Salt, pepper, and seasoning salt to taste

¼ teaspoon garlic powder or fresh garlic to taste

Place cubed eggplant on paper towel and sprinkle with salt. Cover with another paper towel. Let stand while you prepare remaining vegetables.

Heat oil in large skillet until hot. Add onion and garlic and stir-fry until they begin to get tender, about 1 minute. Add eggplant and zucchini and stir-fry until barely tender, about 2 to 3 minutes. You may have to add more oil as the eggplant absorbs it. Add tomatoes and stir-fry until just heated through, about 1 minute more. Season with salt, pepper, and seasoning salt.

Editor's Note: Small, fresh garden eggplant shouldn't need peeling.

SERVES 6.

Sun-Dried Tomatoes with Cucumber

....

Deanne Adams
Vancouver, Washington

½ cup dried tomatoes

2 four- or five-inch sprigs fresh rosemary or ½ teaspoon dry rosemary leaves, lightly crushed to release flavor

2 cloves garlic

½ cup olive oil

¼ teaspoon black pepper

1 cup hot water

1 seven-inch cucumber

Blanch tomatoes in hot water 20 to 30 minutes. Strip leaves from 1 sprig fresh rosemary; chop. Add rosemary, garlic, and pepper to olive oil. Drain tomatoes and add to seasoned oil. Let stand at least 4 hours at room temperature (refrigerate if made ahead more than four hours).

Peel cucumber if necessary. Thin strips of skin left on commercial cucumbers will add to color of dish. Fresh homegrown cucumber need not be peeled. Slice ¼-inch thick in diagonal slices 2 to 3 inches long. Arrange tomato slices on top and pour marinade over. Garnish serving plate with remaining rosemary.

SERVES 4.

———————— ❧ ————————

Rosemary's pretty blue flowers can be used as well as—or in addition to—its leaves.

Peches Negra
Poached peaches with blackberry sauce

....

Don and Evelyn Belloff
Friday Harbor, Washington

Around our house, sugar is considered unhealthy, whereas fructose provides sweetening without adding taste, is safe and convenient to use, and contains fiber so is absorbed slowly without upsetting the blood sugar level. We devote considerable effort toward using this healthy sugar substitute to make tasty desserts that are also good nutritionally. These recipes were created specifically to use San Juan Island produce in a healthy and tasty manner. Only a taste test will reveal just how successful we were.

1 peach

1 cup water

⅓ cup fructose

1 teaspoon vanilla

¼ cup Blackberry Syrup (see recipe below)

½ teaspoon kirschwasser (optional)

¼ cup chilled whipping cream

2 teaspoons powdered fructose (A small food processor is useful to powder regular fructose

1 teaspoon vanilla

8 whole fresh blackberries

BLACKBERRY SYRUP (2 CUPS)

1 pound fresh-picked Himalaya blackberries, washed under a hard spray and drained

1¼ cup fructose or 1 pound sugar

2 tablespoons water

Dip peach in boiling water for 15 seconds and then briefly dip in cold water. Peel, halve, and remove pit. Bring water and fructose to boil in a heavy saucepan over medium-high heat. Cook, stirring, until fructose dissolves. Remove from heat and stir in vanilla. Add peach halves, return to heat, and simmer, covered, for 10 to 20 minutes or until peaches are barely tender. Remove from heat, cool, and then refrigerate.

To make blackberry syrup, place berries in a heavy 2-quart saucepan. Pour fructose and water over and place pan on medium heat. As soon as mixture begins to cook, crush berries with a potato masher and stir. Continue crushing and stirring occasionally until mixture begins to boil. Remove from heat and strain through a sieve, pressing as much pulp through as possible. Bottle and refrigerate. The syrup is good over ice cream, poached fruit, brownies, and on breakfast pancakes, waffles, and French toast.

Variation: Substitute other types of blackberries or raspberries for the Himalayas.

Drain peaches and transfer halves to chilled dessert dishes or champagne glasses. The syrup can be saved to use again. Add kirschwasser (if used) to blackberry syrup and pour over peach halves.

Whip cream in a chilled bowl until it begins to thicken. Sprinkle powdered fructose on top, add vanilla, and beat until cream holds soft peaks. Spoon over syrup and garnish with blackberries.

SERVES 2.

Any Berry Ice

Diana Anderson
Enumclaw, Washington

This is especially good, and a beautiful bright red, with fresh raspberries from the garden.

1 quart puréed berries

½ cup sugar

1 cup water

1 tablespoon lemon juice

Combine berries with sugar and let stand for 2 hours. Force through sieve. Add water and lemon juice. Chill. Freeze in ice cream maker.

MAKES ABOUT 1 QUART.

Cheesy Onion-Zucchini Bake

Lois Golik
Woodland, Washington

3 cups thinly sliced onion rings
(1 large onion)

3 cups thinly sliced zucchini

2 tablespoons butter or margarine

2 eggs, beaten

½ cup sour cream or yogurt

1 teaspoon salt

⅛ teaspoon pepper

½ teaspoon dry mustard

1 cup grated Swiss cheese

Preheat oven to 375°F. Sauté onion and zucchini in butter or margarine until tender. Place in shallow 1½-quart baking dish. Combine eggs, sour cream, salt, pepper, mustard, and half the cheese. Pour over vegetables. Sprinkle with remaining cheese. Bake 20 minutes or until firm.

SERVES 6.

Pinch out any flower stems on young onion plants to prevent bolting.

Zucchini-Rice Casserole

·····································

Deanne Adams
Vancouver, Washington

¼ pound lean ground beef

¼ pound pepperoni (1-inch diameter), diced fine

4 eight-inch zucchini, split lengthwise

½ cup diced sweet onion

¼ cup diced carrot

2 tablespoons chopped fresh tarragon

2 tablespoons chopped fresh parsley

1 teaspoon each fresh thyme leaves,
marjoram, and oregano

1 teaspoon seasoning salt

3 cups cooked short-grain brown rice

1 tablespoon olive oil

½ cup each shredded Cheddar and
Monterey jack cheese

Preheat oven to 375°F. Scoop about ½-inch of seeded center out of zucchini. Chop scoopings and reserve. Spread olive oil across cut surfaces of zucchini halves. Place zucchini in a 9-by-13-inch casserole and heat in oven while preparing rice mix.

Quickly sauté ground beef and pepperoni. Add onion, carrot, herbs, and seasoning salt. Sauté until vegetables are slightly softened. Add chopped zucchini pulp and mix well. Stir in rice and mix again.

Remove zucchini from casserole. Spread a layer of rice mix in casserole and cover with zucchini. Spread remaining rice mix on top. Sprinkle with cheese. Cover with spray-coated aluminum foil. Bake until zucchini is tender.

Note: All vegetables and herbs may be fresh or frozen.

SERVES 6.

Curried Zucchini Soup

Ferne Supler
Edmonds, Washington

6 small zucchini, trimmed and cut
   in chunks

1 cup thinly sliced onion

2 teaspoons curry powder

2 teaspoons sugar

½ teaspoon ground ginger

½ teaspoon dry mustard

3 cups chicken broth or bouillon

3 tablespoons uncooked rice

1½ cups milk (skim, whole,
   or even cream)

Salt and pepper to taste

Dill weed or chopped chives
   (optional)

Combine zucchini, onion, curry powder, sugar, ginger, and mustard in covered saucepan. Add broth and rice. Simmer, covered, 45 minutes. Purée in blender, food processor, or strainer. If in a blender, do a quarter of the mixture at a time. Place in a large bowl and add salt, pepper, and milk or cream. Chill thoroughly or serve hot. Garnish with dill or chives, if desired.

MAKES 7 OR 8 CUPS.

Fettuccine with Zucchini Almond Sauce

······································

Deanne Adams
Vancouver, Washington

2 tablespoons butter

3 cups diced zucchini

1 cup chopped onion

1 clove garlic, crushed

1 cup tomato sauce

1 cup diced tomato

¼ cup chopped green pepper

1 tablespoon chopped fresh tarragon

1 teaspoon chopped fresh rosemary
    leaves

1 teaspoon sugar

½ teaspoon salt

1 pound whole wheat fettuccine

¾ cup chopped or slivered toasted
    almonds

Melt butter in skillet. Add zucchini, onion, and garlic. Cook until zucchini is crisp-tender. Add tomato sauce, tomato, green pepper, tarragon, rosemary, sugar, and salt. Bring to simmer and cook about 15 minutes, until hot and well combined.

Cook fettuccine al dente. Transfer to serving platter, top with sauce, and sprinkle with almonds.

Variation: Even better than whole wheat fettuccine is corn spaghetti.

SERVES 4.

Zucchini Soup

··

Mrs. Donald R. Jopp
Lakebay, Washington

1 medium onion, chopped

2 tablespoons butter or margarine

6 cups sliced zucchini

1½ cups chicken broth

1 teaspoon curry powder

Salt to taste

Sauté onion in butter or margarine. Add zucchini, simmer until soft in part of broth, and then add remainder of broth, curry powder, and salt. Put in blender and blend until smooth. Serve hot or cold.

This recipe was given to me by my sister, Mrs. Patrick Brigham, of Galway, New York.

Editor's Note: If you like the flavor of giblet stock, try it with this recipe.

SERVES 4.

Hot or Chilled Zucchini Soup

·······································

Sieglinde Thatcher
Corvallis, Oregon

Since I never thought I would ever pass these recipes on, I do not have exact measurements as I cook by whatever feels right and smells right.

8 double handfuls peeled, cubed zucchini

½ cup water

8 large fresh basil leaves, chopped or processed

2 tablespoons honey or 2 packets sugar substitute

1 teaspoon onion powder

Salt and pepper (easy on the pepper since the basil is pungent)

Heat water, basil, and honey, add remaining ingredients, and cook about 15 minutes or until zucchini is soft. Liquefy in blender and pour into freezer bags. Leave overnight at room temperature and then chill in refrigerator before freezing.

MAKES ABOUT 1 QUART.

Jones Landing Zucchini

· ·

J. Yvonne Jones
Umpqua, Oregon

4 slices bacon

4 cups sliced small zucchini

½ cup chopped onion

½ teaspoon salt

Pepper

1 tablespoon minced fresh basil or
   1 teaspoon dried

1 egg, beaten

2 tomatoes, chopped

1 or 2 cups grated Cheddar cheese

Cook bacon in skillet until very crisp. Drain, crumble, and set aside. Discard all but 1 tablespoon bacon fat. Add zucchini, onion, salt, pepper, and basil. Lower heat and cook, covered, until almost tender—about 5 to 7 minutes. Quickly add egg to bind juices. Distribute tomato and cheese over zucchini and top with crumbled bacon. Cover for 2 or 3 minutes until tomatoes are heated through and cheese is melted.

SERVES 4 AS A MAIN DISH,
6 AS A SIDE DISH.

Lina's Zucchini (or Carrot) Bread

Lina Gallagher
Seattle, Washington

3 eggs

1 cup salad oil

2 cups sugar

2 teaspoons vanilla

2 cups shredded zucchini or carrots

1 can (8 ounces) crushed pineapple , well drained

2 teaspoons baking soda

1 teaspoon salt

½ teaspoon baking powder

2 teaspoons cinnamon

1 cup chopped walnuts

3 cups flour

1 cup raisins

Preheat oven to 350°F. Beat eggs. Add oil, sugar, and vanilla and beat until light and foamy. Stir in zucchini or carrots and pineapple. Sift together dry ingredients and gently stir into zucchini mixture. Add nuts and raisins.

Pour batter into two greased and floured 5-by-9-inch bread pans. Bake 1 hour or until bread tests done with toothpick. Cool in pans for 10 minutes.

Try to beat off all your new-found friends as you take your first QUALITY CONTROL bite. Enjoy!!!

Editor's Note: This is popular bread. Kathy Lofquist of Eatonville, Washington, submitted the same recipe plus cloves, minus raisins. Nicole Hueffed of Seattle sent the same recipe sans pineapple.

MAKES 2 LOAVES.

Pieggles' Tomato-Zucchini

· ·

Celia Kircher
Dayton, Oregon

Olive oil

1 clove garlic, chopped

1 medium onion, chopped

3 medium zucchini, diced

4 tomatoes, diced

3 or 4 tablespoons fresh basil

Parmesan cheese

Heat olive oil in skillet. Add garlic and onion and cook until soft. Add zucchini and tomatoes, cover, and cook over medium heat until soft. Sprinkle with grated Parmesan and heat until cheese melts. Serve immediately.

SERVES 3 OR 4.

Scalloped Zucchini

· ·

Janice Soderberg
Bellingham, Washington

4 medium zucchini, sliced into ¼-inch thick rounds

Salt, pepper, and nutmeg

1 cup fine bread or cracker crumbs

1½ cups grated Monterey jack cheese

2 cups milk

1 teaspoon butter

Preheat oven to 350°F. Layer one-third of the zucchini in a buttered casserole. Season to taste with salt, pepper, and nutmeg. Cover with one-third of the crumbs and one-third of the cheese. Continue for two more layers. Pour milk over and bake, uncovered, for 35 minutes or until bubbling and golden.

SERVES 4 TO 6.

Plain but Tasty!! Zucchini Stew

John T. Waterman
Sutherlin, Oregon

Delicious served hot and leftover may be frozen for future meals. Handy and economical way to utilize bountiful crops from your garden.

2 cups chicken or turkey broth

5 medium tomatoes, sliced thick and halved

5 medium onions, sliced thick and quartered

3 large unpeeled zucchini, sliced thick

Fresh or powdered garlic to taste

Oregano or other seasonings to taste

Place ingredients in 1-gallon pot, bring to light boil, and cook, covered, for about an hour. Add seasonings to taste.

SERVES 6 TO 8.

Collachi Cheese

Faye Treadaway
Deadwood, Oregon

1 large onion, chopped

2 tablespoons cooking oil

6 or 7 zucchini, unpeeled and sliced thin

1 small can white kernel corn, drained

1 can (4 ounces) green chiles

3 large tomatoes, skinned and chopped

½ pound mild Cheddar cheese, grated

Salt, pepper, and garlic powder

Sauté onion in oil. Add remaining ingredients except cheese. Simmer until zucchini is done and then add cheese until melted and blended.

SERVES 4.

Squash Casserole

· ·

Janice Baker (a nurse who would rather cook for a living)
Eugene, Oregon

This is a great dish (I made it up).

Olive oil

3 medium summer squash—
zucchini, crookneck, etc.—
(about 2 pounds), sliced

1 large onion, sliced in half moons

4 or 5 cloves garlic, minced or put
through a press

Salt and pepper

2 eggs

¾ cup soy milk or dairy milk

½ pound soy cheese

Parmesan cheese

Garlic powder

Thyme

Whole wheat bread crumbs

Paprika

Tomato slices (optional)

Preheat oven to 350°F. Heat olive oil and sauté squash, onion, and garlic until crisp-tender. Season with salt and pepper. Put in casserole dish and top with soy cheese, Parmesan, garlic powder, thyme, and most of the bread crumbs. Beat together eggs and soy milk or dairy milk and pour over casserole layers. Top the whole thing with more bread crumbs, paprika, and tomato slices (if used). Bake, uncovered, for 45 minutes.

SERVES 4 OR 5.

Summer Cheese Bake 1

· ·

Mollie M. Hughes
Arlington, Washington

My favorite garden recipe is simply layering slices of zucchini, peeled tomatoes, and Monterey jack cheese, ending with a layer of cheese on top. I sprinkle basil on each layer of tomatoes. Bake at 350°F, covered, approximately 30 minutes or until zucchini tests tender with a fork. The size or number of layers depends on garden bounty, number of people to feed, etc.

There are lots of variations with the above, but I prefer the flavor created by this version.

Summer Cheese Bake 2

· ·

Sandra Gilbert
Marysville, Washington

Layer sliced tomatoes, sliced zucchini, and sliced onions (yellow are best) in a lightly oiled baking dish. Sprinkle with salt, pepper, and lots of Parmesan (try a mixture of Asiago, Romano, etc. for variety) and microwave or bake at 350°F until all the vegetables are cooked, about 20 minutes. There will be some liquid from the tomatoes and zucchini as they cook; just drain it off.

I've even added scrambled egg for a tasty summer breakfast. The variations on this seem boundless —sprinkle fresh herbs such as basil, oregano, and thyme.

Summer Zucchini Delight

Sherree Ward
Sequim, Washington

Good served over rice; great served over white fish!

Cook together 6 slices of bacon and half an onion, chopped. When onion is browned and bacon is done, remove and save. Leave some of the bacon grease in pan. Add one small chopped zucchini and cook until slightly tender. Add one or two tomatoes, sliced. When done, add bacon and onion and top with Parmesan cheese.

MAKES ABOUT 1½ CUPS.

Zucchini A-Plus

Pauline O. Sadler
Kirkland, Washington

1 tablespoon olive oil

1 tablespoon margarine

1 pound ground turkey or beef

1 large tomato, chopped

1 large onion, chopped

3 or 4 medium zucchini, sliced thin

Several dashes hot-pepper sauce

Pepper and salt to taste

Parmesan cheese

Heat oil and margarine in a large, heavy saucepan. Add meat and cook, stirring, until it is no longer pink. Add tomato, stir, and cook half a minute. Then add the onion and zucchini. Stir in hot-pepper sauce, pepper, and salt. Cover pan and cook over medium heat until zucchini is just tender. Serve with lots of Parmesan.

SERVES 4.

Zucchini alla Cantiniera

Jane Baier-Nelson
Shaw Island, Washington

This is a recipe from southern Italy. Even those who dislike zucchini or get weary of them seem to relish this dish. It can be a side dish or an appetizer.

5 eight-inch zucchini, cut in ¼-inch
slices, slightly on diagonal

Olive oil

2 large cloves garlic, chopped

3 tablespoons red wine vinegar

10 fresh mint leaves, torn

Salt to taste

Set zucchini slices on a rack or towel in the air or sun to dry. Turn to dry both sides. The beads of moisture should evaporate, leaving a dry surface. Fry the slices flat in a small amount of olive oil. Use high heat so the slices become dark, but not quite burned, on each side.

Toss slices with vinegar, garlic, mint leaves, and salt. These ingredients may be adjusted to taste. Let rest an hour or so, tossing to distribute the flavors, and serve at room temperature.

SERVES 4.

Zucchini and Eggplant Pancakes

Dan and Joyce McGrath
Oregon City, Oregon

Our Dusky eggplants are heavy producers here. We know summer has truly arrived when we eat these!

1 eggplant

1 medium zucchini

1 onion

1 to 3 tablespoons flour

½ teaspoon baking powder

1 egg, beaten

White pepper

Vegetable oil or spray shortening

½ cup salsa

½ cup yogurt

Grate eggplant, toss with salt, and set aside 30 minutes. Meanwhile grate zucchini and onion into a bowl. After 30 minutes, squeeze eggplant dry and add to zucchini/onion mix. Add enough flour to make a thick but not dry batter. Stir in baking powder, egg, and pepper to taste.

Heat skillet greased with oil or spray shortening. Drop batter into skillet with large spoon. Cook until golden, and then turn carefully (they're fragile) and cook other side.

Mix salsa and yogurt together to serve as a sauce over pancakes. I cook down chopped tomatoes with onion, garlic, and chile peppers to make my own salsa.

SERVES 4.

Zucchini and Tomatoes Au Gratin

Lorry Alsip
West Linn, Oregon

You can use any stewed tomatoes. I can mine, an Italian-style recipe. I use Black Beauty zucchini.

3 tablespoons olive oil

1 large onion, chopped

2 pounds zucchini, cut in ¼-inch slices

2 cups Italian stewed tomatoes

½ teaspoon salt (optional)

⅛ teaspoon pepper

¾ cup grated Cheddar cheese

Preheat oven to 375°F. Cook onion in hot oil until golden. Add zucchini and cook slowly, stirring frequently. When zucchini is tender, about 5 to 8 minutes, add tomatoes and their juice and cook, covered, about 5 more minutes. Add salt and pepper.

Spread into greased baking dish. Sprinkle cheese over top and bake about 20 minutes.

SERVES 6 TO 8.

Zucchini Burritos

....

Kathy Ringo
Seattle, Washington

1 or 2 tablespoons oil or cooking fat

1 or 2 cloves garlic, crushed

2 small zucchini, sliced thin

1 large or 2 small carrots, sliced thin

1 medium onion, sliced thin

1 or 2 medium tomatoes (Roma types are best), sliced thin

3 or 4 large mushrooms, sliced thin

¼ to ½ cup salsa

1 package flour tortillas

GARNISHES (TO TASTE)

1 can sliced black olives

2 cups grated Cheddar or Monterey jack cheese

Shredded lettuce

1 avocado, sliced

Yogurt or sour cream

In a large pan, sauté garlic in oil or fat. Add sliced vegetables and sauté in salsa (amount needed depends on how juicy the tomatoes are). Cook over low to medium heat until vegetables are very tender and seasoned by salsa, usually 15 or 20 minutes.

Heat flour tortillas your favorite way (we steam ours on a rack over an inch of water in the Dutch oven). Spread filling on tortillas, roll up tortillas, and garnish as you like. (We cook half the veggie mix one night and the other half the next for our family of three.)

MAKES 10 OR 12 MEDIUM BURRITOS.

Zucchini Crescent Pie

....

Marshall A. Voight
Ferndale, Washington

Even kids like this.

4 cups sliced zucchini

1 cup coarsely chopped onion

¼ cup margarine

½ teaspoon salt

¼ teaspoon pepper

¼ teaspoon garlic powder

1 teaspoon dried basil leaves

¾ teaspoon dried oregano

2 eggs, beaten

2 cups (8 ounces) shredded
    mozzarella cheese

1 can (8 ounces) quick crescent
    dinner rolls

Preheat oven to 375°F. Sauté zucchini and onion in margarine until just tender; set aside. Stir in salt, pepper, garlic powder, basil, and oregano. In a bowl beat eggs; stir in cheese and vegetable mixture.

Separate dough into triangles and press over bottom and sides of ungreased 10-inch pie plate to form crust. Pour vegetable mixture evenly into crust. Bake 20 to 25 minutes or until knife inserted halfway from edge comes out clean. Let stand 10 minutes before serving. Cut into wedges.

MAKES ONE 10-INCH PIE.

Zucchini in Spaghetti Sauce

··

Rhoda Yordy
Lebanon, Oregon

1 pound hamburger

1 zucchini, chopped

Green pepper, shredded

Garlic, minced

1 pint thick home-canned tomato
    juice

Cheddar cheese

Spaghetti sauce seasoning

Brown hamburger in large skillet.
Add zucchini. Continue cooking,
adding a little green pepper and
garlic. Add tomato juice and continue cooking, adding a little cheese
and seasoning. Salt as needed.

Zucchini Italiano

··

Benton G. Williams
Port Orchard, Washington

2 tablespoons olive oil

1 medium onion, chopped

3 or 4 freshly picked small zucchini,
    sliced

1 clove garlic, minced

1 tablespoon fresh oregano

Romano or Parmesan cheese

Salt and pepper

Chop onion and sauté in olive oil.
Add garlic, zucchini, oregano, and
salt and pepper to taste. Cook until zucchini is just tender and firm.
Do not overcook. Place in serving
dish and sprinkle amply with
Parmesan or Romano.

SERVES 2 OR 3.

Zucchini Pancakes

Carol Pryor
Cottage Grove, Oregon

3 cups grated, unpeeled zucchini

½ cup flour

1 egg

1 teaspoon salt

½ teaspoon baking soda

½ cup unsalted sunflower seeds, chopped almonds, or walnuts

Sliced mushrooms or grated Monterey jack or Cheddar cheese

Mix together the zucchini, flour, egg, salt, baking soda, and seeds or nuts. Fry by spoonfuls in skillet until brown. Remove to an oven-proof dish. Top with mushrooms or cheese and heat through in a warm oven.

SERVES 2 OR 3.

Zucchini Frittata

Kate McDermott
Port Angeles, Washington

1 medium-large zucchini, grated

2 cups bread crumbs

1½ cups grated Parmesan cheese

1½ cups olive oil

1 cup fresh or ⅔ cup dried parsley

2 onions, chopped

3 cloves garlic, chopped

1½ tablespoons Italian seasoning

1 teaspoon pepper

1½ teaspoons salt

10 eggs

Mix all together and bake at 325°F for 30 to 40 minutes.

SERVES 6 TO 8.

Zucchini Quiche

....

Sylvia Goheen
Olympia, Washington

Along with a salad, this makes a great nonmeat meal. Heats up quite nicely in the microwave the next day, too.

3 cups grated unpeeled zucchini

1 cup biscuit mix

½ cup olive oil

5 eggs, beaten, or equivalent amount egg substitute

½ cup finely chopped onion

2 tablespoons chopped parsley

½ teaspoon salt (optional)

Dash pepper

½ teaspoon dried marjoram or oregano

1 clove garlic, minced

1 cup grated Parmesan cheese

Preheat oven to 350°F. Mix all ingredients and spread evenly in greased 9-by-13-inch pan. Bake 30 minutes or until golden brown. Cool 5 minutes and cut into small squares for appetizers or larger squares for dinner.

SERVES 4.

Zucchini Haters' Casserole

Mary Rancourt
Eastsound, Washington

Even my young children like this casserole.

3 medium zucchini (about 2
pounds), unpeeled, sliced,
and cooked

½ cup sour cream

2 eggs, slightly beaten

1 onion, diced fine

¾ cup cracker crumbs

1 teaspoon salt

¼ teaspoon pepper

1 cup grated Cheddar cheese

Preheat oven to 350°F. Drain zucchini, let cool slightly, and mash well. Combine with remaining ingredients. Pour into greased casserole. Top with more grated cheese. Bake, uncovered, for 45 minutes.

Note: Don't use Walla Walla sweet onions, as they don't cook down, unless one likes crunchy onions.

SERVES 6 TO 8.

Zucchini Strips

· ·

Dorothy Schmitt
Chehalis, Washington

3 medium zucchini, cut into ½-by-
2-inch strips

2 tablespoons vegetable oil

1 tablespoon dry sherry

¼ cup diced green onions

1 clove garlic, minced

¼ teaspoon salt

⅛ teaspoon crushed red pepper flakes

Put zucchini in a large bowl. In a smaller bowl, stir together vegetable oil, sherry, green onion, garlic salt, and red pepper flakes. Pour over zucchini and toss to coat. Refrigerate, stirring occasionally, until about 5 minutes before serving.

Heat wok or large skillet over high heat. Add zucchini mixture. Stir-fry 3 or 4 minutes, until crisp-tender. Serve immediately.

Note: Zucchini can be marinated several hours. Serve with dressing.

MAKES 3½ CUPS.

Grated Zucchini

· ·

Kate Olson
Banks, Oregon

2 tablespoons butter

2 large zucchini (about 4 pounds),
grated

⅛ teaspoon nutmeg

1 tablespoon lemon juice

Heat butter until bubbly in a heavy skillet. Add zucchini and cook 2 or 3 minutes over high heat, turning once or twice with a spatula. Sprinkle with nutmeg, pour lemon juice over, and simmer a few minutes until zucchini is cooked but still crisp.

SERVES 4.

Zucchini–Ground Beef Casserole

Marshall A. Voight
Ferndale, Washington

This has a crusty, cheese-flavored topping. It can be prepared the day before.

1 pound ground beef

1 medium onion, chopped

1 quart home-canned tomatoes

2 cans (16 ounces total) tomato sauce

1 small green pepper, chopped (optional)

1 cup shredded Cheddar cheese

6 or 7 medium zucchini, sliced ½-inch thick

½ cup black olives, whole or sliced

Salt and pepper

1 clove garlic, minced

¼ teaspoon oregano

½ teaspoon basil

¾ cup Parmesan cheese

Preheat oven to 350°F. Sauté meat and onion. Add tomatoes, tomato sauce, green pepper (if used), Cheddar, zucchini, and olives. Season with salt, pepper, garlic, oregano, and basil. Simmer, uncovered, for 10 minutes. Turn into two 8-inch square pans (for two meals) or one 9-by-13-inch pan. Sprinkle generously with Parmesan. Bake 1 hour or until sauce is thickened and top is nicely browned and crusty.

SERVES 8.

Zucchini Wedding Cake

·····································

Lane Morgan
Sumas, Washington

This creation comes from *The Zucchini Cookbook* by Paula Simmons. Now out of print, it was a Seattle best-seller when it appeared in 1974 and was the inspiration for many other garden cookbooks. I had always intended to have this cake at my wedding, but I ended up getting married in January so it didn't work out.

½ cup vegetable oil

½ cup butter

2 cups sugar

4 cups flour

3 tablespoons cornstarch

1 tablespoon plus 1 teaspoon baking powder

1⅓ cups milk

2 cups finely chopped zucchini

1 teaspoon almond extract

1 teaspoon grated lemon peel

6 egg whites

CANDIED ZUCCHINI

2 pounds sugar

1 lemon, sliced

1 tablespoon vanilla

2 cups water

2½ pounds small zucchini, sliced in ½-inch rounds

Preheat oven to 375°F. Cream together the oil and butter. Add sugar and beat until fluffy. Mix together flour, cornstarch, and baking powder and sift into sugar mixture, alternating with milk. Beat well after each addition. Add almond extract and lemon peel and stir in zucchini. Beat egg whites until stiff and fold gently into batter.

Bake in greased and floured pans for 25 to 30 minutes.

While cakes are baking, make candied zucchini: Combine sugar, lemon, vanilla, and water and bring to boil. Add zucchini and cook until transparent and slightly candied. Drain. The syrup can be reused.

When cakes are cool, decorate as follows: Make double recipe of powdered sugar or boiled icing. Put two-thirds of icing in one bowl and divide remaining third into two smaller bowls. Tint large bowl of icing pale green and make one small bowl medium green and one dark green. Spread tops and sides of all layers with pale green and use darker colors for decorations.

Twist candied zucchini slices and stick into frosting around top edges of each layer. Place zucchini slices flat against frosted sides of layers and put a rosette of darker frosting in the center of each slice.

Place upper cake layers on trimmed sheets of white cardboard. Use small zucchini cut to equal lengths as supporting pillars. Rest bottom of each pillar on a toothpick laid horizontally to keep it from sinking into layer below. To anchor pillars, insert 1 toothpick vertically halfway up into the bottom of each pillar and push the exposed half into the layer beneath.

MAKES A 3-TIERED CAKE.

Fall

Cauliflower-Feta Soup

Jane Becklake
Saltspring Island, British Columbia

This is a thick, creamed soup, good also if eaten the following day. Serve with crisp toast.

1 head cauliflower

Feta cheese

Green onions, chopped

Salt and pepper

Steam cauliflower until soft. Purée, using the water from the steaming to get a thick, souplike consistency. Return purée to low heat and add crumbled feta to taste. Heat until cheese melts. Add salt and pepper to taste and garnish with green onions.

SERVES 4 TO 6.

Cream of Broccoli Soup

Stella Markee
Tillamook, Oregon

1 pound broccoli, cut up fine

3 cups chicken broth

¼ cup flour

2 tablespoons butter or margarine

3½ cups milk

½ cup chopped hominy bits

½ cup half-and-half

½ cup grated Swiss cheese

Cook broccoli in chicken broth until tender. Melt butter or margarine, stir in flour, and add milk. Cook until mixture thickens slightly and then add broccoli and stock, hominy, half-and-half, and Swiss cheese. Heat thoroughly but do not boil. This is very good. Just get it all mixed up and you have a great soup.

SERVES 4 TO 6.

Soupe Au Pistou

....

Marshall Voight
Ferndale, Washington

This is a wonderful end-of-gardening-season recipe. Substitutions are easy and other in-season vegetables can be added.

SOUP

3 quarts water

2 cups diced carrots

2 cups diced boiling potatoes

2 cups chopped onions

1 tablespoon salt

2 cups fresh white beans or 2 cans drained kidney beans

4 or 5 medium zucchini, sliced

2 cups diced green beans

½ cup broken spaghetti

2 large slices sourdough bread, torn into small pieces

¼ teaspoon pepper

PISTOU

4 cloves garlic, mashed

6 tablespoons tomato paste

¼ cup fresh basil or 2 tablespoons dried

½ cup grated Parmesan cheese

¼ to ½ cup olive oil

Put water, carrots, potatoes, onions, salt, and fresh beans (if used) in large pan, bring to boil, and cook 30 to 40 minutes. Twenty minutes before serving, add zucchini, green beans, canned kidney beans (if used), spaghetti, bread, and pepper. While soup is cooking, mix in a large bowl all pistou ingredients except olive oil. With a wooden spoon, slowly beat in olive oil a few drops at a time. Add hot soup to pistou a cup at a time.

Serve with French or sourdough bread.

SERVES 6 TO 8.

Kohlrabi Soup

....

Ann Kosanovic-Brown
Seattle, Washington

2 medium kohlrabi, grated fine

2 tablespoons butter

2 tablespoons flour

1 quart water plus chicken,
vegetable, or beef bouillon
cubes to taste or 1 quart stock—
vegetable or chicken—plus salt

2 tablespoons fresh lemon juice

Sauté kohlrabi in butter until fairly tender. Add flour and stir. Then add stock and simmer for 5 to 10 minutes. Add lemon juice just before serving.

SERVES 4.

Sweet and Sour Broccoli Salad

....

Diana Anderson
Enumclaw, Washington

This is a good way to fix leftover stems after using up the florets.

1 pound broccoli stems

¼ cup vinegar

¼ cup sugar

½ teaspoon salt

2 tablespoons sesame oil

Peel broccoli stems and cut into thin diagonal slices. Combine with vinegar, sugar, and salt. Coat well. Cover and refrigerate overnight, stirring occasionally. Drain and stir in sesame oil just before serving.

SERVES 4.

Sauerkraut Salad

Judy Moilanen
Port Angeles, Washington

1 quart sauerkraut, well drained

1 green pepper, chopped

1 red sweet pepper, chopped

1 medium onion, chopped

2 or 3 carrots, shredded

1 cup celery, chopped

1 teaspoon celery seed

½ cup salad oil

½ cup vinegar

1 cup sugar

Combine vegetables and celery seed. Mix together oil, vinegar, and sugar and add to vegetables. Cover and refrigerate overnight before serving. Keeps indefinitely under refrigeration.

MAKES ABOUT 6 CUPS.

Healthy Salad

Diana Anderson
Enumclaw, Washington

2 cups cauliflower florets

1 cup sliced carrots

2 cups green beans, crisp-cooked

1½ cups bean sprouts

¼ cup shelled sunflower seeds

Combine salad ingredients and toss with Lemon-Yogurt Dressing (Page 29) to taste.

SERVES 4.

Herbed Garden Potato Salad

Karen Pryor
North Bend, Washington

3 pounds thin-skinned new potatoes
(Yellow Finns—yum!)

1 huge sweet onion, chopped fine

3 six-inch sprigs tarragon or oregano

1 three-inch sprig rosemary

6 six-inch sprigs lemon thyme or
regular thyme

6 six-inch sprigs Italian parsley
or cilantro

6 six-inch sprigs regular parsley

½ cup red wine vinegar

2 teaspoons salt

1 tablespoon Dijon mustard

1½ cups light olive oil or peanut oil

Poach potatoes in hot water until just done. Slice thin. Put potatoes and onion in a big bowl. Pick off herb leaves and discard stems. Chop leaves in blender or food processor or chop fine by hand. Combine vinegar, salt, mustard, and oil in a bowl, add herbs and mix. Pour this dressing over potatoes and onion and mix thoroughly. (Mix with your hands to keep potato slices whole.) Let sit at room temperature an hour or so, to absorb flavors. (No eggs or mayonnaise, so it can't spoil. You can carry it in the car at this point.)

Before serving, stir in some chopped spinach, sorrel, chives, or whatever you have in the garden that's green, for color. Serve at room temperature.

Variation: You can make this into a main dish by adding 3 pounds smoked German or Polish sausage—sliced, browned in a frying pan, and drained—before serving.

SERVES 12 OR MORE.

———— 🌿 ————

Pigweed and potato are good companion plants.

Turnip and Carrot Slaw

Lois M. Burrow
Seaford, Delaware

4 cups grated turnips

2 cups grated carrots

1 Bermuda onion, chopped

¾ cup sugar

1 cup cider vinegar

½ cup oil

1 teaspoon celery seed

1 teaspoon dry mustard

1 teaspoon salt

Toss turnips, carrots, and onions together in a bowl. Combine sugar, vinegar, oil, celery seed, mustard, and salt in a bowl and bring to a boil. Pour over vegetables.

Editor's Note: Lois Burrow is co-author of *Too Many Tomatoes and Other Good Things: A Cookbook for When Your Garden Explodes.* This recipe is from the book.

SERVES 6 TO 8.

Turnips and rutabagas have an odor that affects celery in storage. Keep them apart.

Broccoli Vinaigrette

Jana Drobinsky
El Cerrito, California

From *Compliments of the Chef,* a cookbook put out by the Sisterhood of Beth El Congregation, Berkeley, California, using recipes from local restaurants. This one comes from Curds and Whey, a deli which is no longer in business. This sauce can be used on broccoli alone, or over a platter of mixed lightly steamed vegetables. We usually use broccoli, green and red peppers, green beans, snap peas, etc.—whatever is fresh.

1 cup or less peanut oil

¼ cup red wine vinegar

2 tablespoons lemon juice

Freshly ground black pepper

1 tablespoon soy sauce

¼ cup Dijon mustard

*¼ to ½ cup toasted almonds,
sunflower seeds, or sesame seeds*

Blend together all but the almonds or seeds. Pour dressing over vegetables. Top with nuts or seeds.

MAKES A PLATTER FOR 6 OR APPETIZERS FOR 12.

Cabbages, broccoli, and Brussels sprouts are all big, top-heavy plants and they like a firm (though rich) soil. Don't waste your double digging on them. Save it for the carrots. Onions are another shallow-rooted plant that needs firm soil.

Bavarian Kohlrabi

Cheryl Boden
Union Gardens, Hillsboro, Oregon

6 three-inch kohlrabi

2 tablespoons butter

2 tablespoons flour

1 or 2 teaspoons caraway seed

1 cup milk

Salt and pepper to taste

Parsley for garnish

Peel and cut kohlrabi into thick julienne strips. Steam until tender. While kohlrabi is cooking, melt butter in heavy saucepan, whisk in flour and caraway seed, and cook over low heat for a minute or two (don't brown the flour). Whisk in milk gradually and stir just until smooth and thickened. Combine sauce and steamed kohlrabi, add salt and pepper to taste, and stir to coat. Garnish with chopped parsley and serve.

SERVES 6.

Kohlrabi should be harvested when enlarged stems have become 1½ to 3 inches in diameter. If they are allowed to become larger they get tough and stringy.

Broccoli Casserole

....

Garland Ross
Gold Hill, Oregon

¼ to ⅓ cup margarine

¼ cup chopped onion

1 large bag broccoli or equivalent
 fresh, cooked until almost done

1 cup stuffing crumbs

2 eggs

1 can mushroom soup

½ cup mayonnaise

1 cup grated Cheddar cheese

Preheat oven to 350°F. Sauté onions in margarine. Mix with remaining ingredients and put in casserole dish. Bake 35 to 45 minutes or until knife comes out clean.

SERVES 3 OR 4.

Broccoli with Garlic

....

Hannah Salia
Seattle, Washington

I use the Hybrid Broccoli Blend for this.

2 or 3 large bunches broccoli

3 to 5 large cloves garlic

Olive oil

Parmesan cheese

Parboil broccoli for 5 minutes or until just tender. Chop garlic fine. Heat enough oil in heavy skillet to lightly coat broccoli. Add garlic and sauté until golden brown. Add broccoli and coat with oil and garlic, turning occasionally, for about 5 or 6 minutes or until heated through. Toss with Parmesan to taste. Delicious! Even kids love it.

SERVES 4 TO 6.

Gado-Gado

Steamed vegetables with spicy Indonesian sauce

Kayla M. Starr
Cave Junction, Oregon

SAUCE

2 tablespoons butter, margarine, or
  peanut oil

1 cup minced onion

3 cloves garlic, minced

1 large bay leaf

2 or more teaspoons grated fresh
  ginger

1 cup smooth peanut butter

1 tablespoon honey

1 tablespoon vinegar

1 tablespoon hot-pepper sesame oil or
  ¼ to ½ teaspoon cayenne pepper

1 teaspoon tamari or soy sauce

Juice of 1 lemon

3 cups water

VEGETABLES

Broccoli florets

Carrots, sliced lengthwise

Green beans

Potato chunks

Large kale or chard stems

Fried tofu or tempeh (optional)

Heat butter, margarine, or oil in
large pot. Add onion, garlic, bay
leaf, and ginger and sauté. Then
add peanut butter, honey, vinegar,
hot oil or cayenne, tamari or soy
sauce, lemon juice, and water. Mix
and simmer 30 minutes. While
sauce is cooking, steam vegetables
until barely tender. Arrange on a
platter with tofu or tempeh (if
used) and pour sauce over.

SERVES 6.

Green Tomato Bread

....

Torchy Oberg
Forest Grove, Oregon

A good way to use some of the green tomatoes when we have those summers that don't last long enough to ripen the last of the tomatoes.

*2 pounds ground or finely chopped
   green tomatoes*

3 eggs

1 cup oil

2 cups sugar

2 teaspoons vanilla

1 teaspoon soda

2 rounded teaspoons cinnamon

¾ teaspoon salt

¼ teaspoon baking powder

3 cups flour

*1 cup ground or chopped nuts
   (optional)*

1 cup raisins (optional)

Pour boiling water over tomatoes and then drain. Repeat procedure twice and then measure out 2 cups tomatoes.

Preheat oven to 325°F. Beat eggs until light and fluffy. Add oil, sugar, ground tomatoes, and vanilla. Beat well. Add dry ingredients and mix until well blended. Bake 1 to 1½ hours. Cool before slicing.

Editor's Note: The boiling water treatment renders the tomatoes virtually invisible in the bread. If you want more tomato presence you can reserve half a cup of chopped, seeded, tomatoes from the boiling water treatment.

MAKES 2 LOAVES.

Green Tomato Parmesan

Charles Williamson
Gig Harbor, Washington

3 tablespoons olive oil, divided

1 onion, coarsely chopped

1 green pepper, coarsely chopped

6 to 8 mushrooms, chopped

2 or 3 cloves garlic, crushed or
chopped fine

1 teaspoon sugar

¼ teaspoon oregano

½ teaspoon basil

12 to 15 medium green tomatoes,
sliced

2 or 3 large eggs

1 cup flour

4 cups (1 pound) grated Muenster
cheese

Parmesan cheese

Preheat oven to 350°F. Heat 1 tablespoon olive oil in saucepan. Add onion and sauté until soft. Add green pepper, mushrooms, garlic, sugar, and herbs and cook over low heat until tender. Meanwhile, dip tomato slices in flour and then in beaten eggs. Heat remaining olive oil in skillet and brown tomato slices. Set aside.
In a casserole dish, put a layer of sauce, followed by a layer of tomatoes topped with Muenster cheese. Repeat layers until all tomatoes are used. Top with Parmesan and bake 40 minutes.

SERVES 6 TO 8.

Store green tomatoes so the fruits don't touch. One way is to wrap each tomato in a sheet of newspaper. Keep them in a cool, dry place and check frequently. The reason you don't pile them together is that one rotten tomato can quickly ruin its neighbors.

Taylors' Horticultural Beans

....

Janet Boyce
Ellensburg, Washington

Use fresh or frozen beans. I don't dry them, but shell them when they are mature.

Simmer or steam beans with chopped onion and a little celery. When tender, add butter, salt, and pepper. Wonderful!

My Recipe

....

Phyllis Vallade
Seattle, Washington

A couple of carrots

Some broccoli

A handful of green beans

1 can cream of chicken or cream of mushroom soup

Beans dry nicely on the vine, and vine-dried beans are much easier to shell, but in damp maritime autumns they often rot instead of drying. Wait as long as you can, preferably until pods are dry but at least until they are pliable. Then shell them. (Don't delay; mold spreads fast in a pile of damp pods.) Then dry them until hard in a food dryer, warm oven, over a heat vent, or wherever. Some books tell you to blanch before drying, but it isn't necessary.

Cook vegetables a little and drain. Heat soup and mix with vegetables. Toss together. If wanted, add a little cheese and heat in microwave oven. For a larger family, add more vegetables and thin soup with a little milk.

SERVES 2.

Nanny's Broccoli and Macaroni

Joanne Liantonio
La Conner, Washington

This is a recipe from my Italian grandmother.

¾ cup olive oil

1 pound pasta—preferably tube shape, such as ziti, rigatoni, mostaccioli

¾ pound fresh broccoli, cut into thick spears

½ cup chopped onion

1 large clove garlic, minced

Herbs to taste—oregano, basil, parsley

2 cups bread crumbs

Salt and pepper to taste

⅓ cup grated Romano or Parmesan cheese

Bring large pot of water to a boil. Add salt (optional) and 1 teaspoon of the oil, and then add pasta. About 4 or 5 minutes before pasta is done, add broccoli spears. Boil until the pasta is done and broccoli just tender. Drain.

Meanwhile, heat remaining oil in a skillet. Sauté onions and garlic until transparent. Add herbs, bread crumbs, salt, and pepper and fry until golden. Toss bread crumb mixture with broccoli and pasta. Top with sprinkle of grated cheese. Serve hot.

SERVES 4 HUNGRY FOLKS OR 5 NORMAL PEOPLE.

Broccoli likes cool feet. If you have to grow it in hot weather, use a heavy mulch.

Sesame Cauliflower

J. Yvonne Jones
Umpqua, Oregon

1 head cauliflower

1 quart reconstituted dry skim milk
   (optional)

Sauce (recipe below)

2 tablespoons sesame seeds, toasted

SAUCE

2 tablespoons butter

2 tablespoons flour

1 cup chicken broth

1 teaspoon lemon juice

Cook whole cauliflower in boiling water or milk (if used). Cooking in milk keeps cauliflower white and prevents the breakdown of the sulfur compounds that give that "cabbagey" smell. Simmer at just under boiling point for 20 minutes or until just tender. Place on serving platter, cover with sauce, and serve immediately. The sauce can be prepared ahead of time and reheated.

To make the sauce, melt butter in medium saucepan, stir in flour, and gradually stir in broth. Cook, stirring constantly, until mixture thickens. Gently stir in lemon juice and salt. Spoon over cauliflower. Sprinkle with toasted sesame seeds.

SERVES 6.

Vegetable Barley

· ·

Steve Lower
Bear Wallow Farm, Mad River, California

Colorfully full of vegetables, this dish is especially quick to prepare if you have leftover rice or barley. It's best if all ingredients are fresh from your garden.

1¼ cups raw barley or rice

2 tablespoons soy grits

2 teaspoons salt

¼ cup oil

2 cups sliced carrots

1 large onion, sliced

2 stalks celery, chopped

1 green pepper, chopped

1½ cups chopped mushrooms

*2 teaspoons freshly ground coriander
    seeds*

2 teaspoons ground dill seeds

Cook together the barley or rice, soy grits, and salt. Meanwhile, heat oil in large frying pan or wok. Sauté vegetables in order given, adding each one as the one before gets hot and starts to sizzle. Total cooking time should be about 10 minutes. The carrots should be crisp, the onions lightly browned, the celery and green pepper crisp, and the mushrooms browned. Stir in the dill and coriander, and then add cooked barley and soy grits. Brown barley slightly with cooked vegetables. Serve at once.

SERVES 6.

Apple Crisp

Maxine Fritz
Canby, Oregon

4 cups sliced cooking apples

1 tablespoon lemon juice

⅓ cup flour

½ cup firmly packed brown sugar

½ teaspoon salt

1 teaspoon cinnamon

⅓ cup melted butter or margarine

Preheat oven to 375°F. Place sliced apples in a shallow pan. Sprinkle with lemon juice. Combine dry ingredients and add melted butter, mixing until crumbly. Sprinkle crumb mixture over apples. Bake 30 minutes or until apples are tender.

Variation: Use berries instead of apples. Omit lemon juice and cinnamon.

SERVES 6.

Popcorn should not be harvested until the ears have matured fully. The silks need to be dry and withered and the husks should be turning straw color. The kernels should be very firm. Cut each ear with about 1½ to 2 inches of stalk below the ear. Strip back the husks (leaving them attached) and hang to dry completely. When they are thoroughly dry, the kernels can be removed and stored in jars.

Apple Muffins

....

Linda Lowber
Kent, Washington

½ cup apple juice

⅓ cup sugar

¼ cup oil

1 egg

1½ cups flour

2 teaspoons baking powder

½ teaspoon cinnamon

¼ teaspoon salt

1 cup chopped peeled apples

TOPPING

⅓ cup chopped walnuts

1 tablespoon packed brown sugar

½ teaspoon cinnamon

Preheat oven to 350°F. Combine apple juice, sugar, oil, and egg and blend well. In a separate bowl combine flour, baking powder, cinnamon, and salt. Add liquid to dry ingredients, stirring just until blended. Fold in apples. Divide batter among 10 muffin cups. Combine topping ingredients and sprinkle over batter. Bake 20 minutes or until toothpick inserted in center comes out clean.

MAKES 10 MUFFINS.

Apple Roll

···

Virginia Lacy
Auburn, Washington

Better than apple pie!

2 or 3 large apples, peeled and diced

½ cup sugar

DOUGH

2 cups flour

3 tablespoons sugar

2 teaspoons baking powder

1 teaspoon salt

¾ cup shortening

½ cup milk

SYRUP

1½ cups sugar

2 cups water

3 tablespoons butter

¼ teaspoon nutmeg

½ teaspoon cinnamon

Mix apples and sugar and set aside. Combine syrup ingredients in saucepan and bring to boil. Meanwhile, combine dry ingredients for dough. Cut in shortening and then add milk. Roll out dough as for a jelly roll but not too thin. Spread apple mixture along one edge, roll up the dough, seal edges, and slice into spirals. Place slices in 9-by-13-inch pan and pour hot syrup over all. Bake 30 minutes. Serve warm.

SERVES 6.

Grandmother's Norwegian Apple Pie

Mrs. Betty Ruiter

1 cup sugar

1 cup flour

½ teaspoon salt

½ teaspoon baking powder

2 eggs

1 teaspoon apple pie spice mixture

1 cup chopped nuts

2 cups diced apples

Preheat oven to 350°F. Combine sugar, flour, salt, baking powder, and spices. Beat eggs into dry ingredients, and then stir in nuts and apples. This makes a very stiff batter. Press the batter into a 9-inch pie pan and bake 30 minutes.

MAKES ONE 9-INCH PASTRY.

Raw Apple Cake

···

Debra Gillis-Berlin
Astoria, Oregon

This cake can sit out uncovered and it will not dry out (if it lasts that long).

2 cups sugar

1 cup butter or margarine

2 eggs

1 cup orange juice

2 teaspoons vanilla

2½ cups flour

½ teaspoon salt

1 tablespoon cinnamon

2 teaspoons baking soda

4 cups chopped raw apples

1 cup chopped nuts

Preheat oven to 350°F. Cream together sugar, butter, and eggs. Blend in orange juice and vanilla. Mix dry ingredients together, then add them to creamed mixture. Stir in apples and nuts. Spread into greased 9-by-13-inch pan. Bake 90 minutes or until done.

Variations: You can play with the ingredients by adding different spices, raisins, coconut, and extra apples.

MAKES ONE 9-BY-13-INCH CAKE.

Pear Clafouti

. . . .

Linda Lowber
Kent, Washington

3 eggs

1¼ cups milk

½ cup flour

⅓ cup sugar

2 teaspoons vanilla

¼ teaspoon rum extract

⅛ teaspoon salt

⅛ teaspoon ground nutmeg

3 medium pears, peeled, cored, and
chopped, or one can (29 ounces)
pears, drained well and chopped

Whipped cream

Preheat oven to 350°F. Beat eggs until foamy. Add milk, flour, sugar, vanilla, rum extract, salt, and nutmeg. Beat at low speed until smooth. Spread pears in greased 10-inch quiche dish or pie plate. Pour batter over pears. Bake 50 to 60 minutes or until knife inserted in center comes out clean. Let stand 15 minutes. Garnish with whipped cream.

Editor's Note: Clafoutis also are excellent made with apples, peaches, or blueberries.

SERVES 8.

Rose Hip Pie

Marian Glenz
Meyers Chuck, Alaska

This makes a custardy filling dotted with red hips. Very rich. A little lemon juice keeps it from becoming too blah.

1½ tablespoons cornstarch

1 cup sugar

¼ cup melted margarine

2 eggs, beaten

1 cup light corn syrup

Dash salt

1 teaspoon vanilla

Lemon juice (optional)

2 or 3 cups halved, seeded rosehips

Pastry for double-crust 9-inch pie

Preheat oven to 350°F. Mix together cornstarch, sugar, and margarine. Add eggs, corn syrup, salt, vanilla, and lemon juice (if used). Stir in rosehips. Pour into pie shell. Cover with lattice crust. Bake 35 to 40 minutes or until custard is set.

MAKES ONE 9-INCH PIE.

Shelly's Birthday Cake

....

Sky Groth
Emeryville, California

Before it was Shelly's cake, it was Kathy Getty's mother's apple cake. It can be doubled or even tripled easily.

1 cup chopped walnuts or hazelnuts or mixture

2 cups chopped apples

1 egg

1 cup sugar, brown and white together

¼ cup corn, salad, or canola oil

1 cup flour

1 teaspoon baking soda

1 teaspoon cinnamon

¼ teaspoon cloves

¼ teaspoon nutmeg

Preheat oven to 350°F. Mix together in a large bowl the nuts, apples, egg, sugar, and oil. Sift dry ingredients together and add to apple-nut mixture. Pour batter in a greased 8-by-8-inch pan and bake 30 minutes. Test with toothpick to make sure apples are done.

Variation: Replace the sugar and oil in the recipe with ½ cup brown sugar, ¼ cup honey, and ¼ cup melted butter. Increase flour by 2 to 4 tablespoons.

MAKES ONE SQUARE CAKE.

Special Blueberry Muffins

Linda Lowber
Kent, Washington

2 cups sifted flour

2 teaspoons baking powder

½ teaspoon salt

½ cup butter

1¼ cups sugar

2 eggs

½ cup milk

2½ cups blueberries

Preheat oven to 350°F. Grease muffin pan. Sift flour with baking powder and salt and set aside. In large bowl, cream butter with sugar until light and fluffy. Add eggs, one at a time, beating well after each addition. Add flour mixture alternately with milk, beating by hand until just combined.

With fork, mash ½ cup berries. Stir into batter with fork, add the rest of the whole berries, and mix gently.

Fill muffin tins three-quarters full. Sprinkle each with sugar. Bake 25 to 30 minutes, or until lightly browned. Let cool in tins 15 minutes, remove, and serve warm.

MAKES 12 MUFFINS.

Sugarless Blueberry Pie

Dorothy Simmons
Bremerton, Washington

PIE CRUST

1½ cups Grapenuts cereal

¼ cup apple juice concentrate

FILLING

1 cup apple juice concentrate

*¼ cup water mixed with 3 table-
spoons cornstarch*

2 cups fresh or frozen blueberries

2 teaspoons orange rind

Mix crust ingredients until
Grapenuts are moist. (I use a food
processor; it's faster.) Press into pie
dish and set aside.

Combine concentrate with
cornstarch and water mixture in a
small saucepan. Mix and cook over
medium heat until thick and transparent. Remove from heat and add
blueberries and orange rind. Pour
into pie shell. Cover with whipped
cream. Let chill 1 hour.

Variation: For the family I double recipe. Place Grapenuts mix in
9-by-13-inch pan. Stretch blueberries with 2 large apples, diced.
Cover with foil and bake at 350°F
for 40 minutes. When apples are
tender, double apple juice/corn-
starch mix. Cook on stove top until thick and transparent. Pour over
hot fruit and spread about. We eat
it without topping and the children come back for seconds.

Editor's Note: If you make
your own cider you can also
make your own concentrate.
Freeze cider in a plastic gallon
jug, leaving some room for the
liquid to expand. Remove container from freezer and place upside-down in a large bowl. The
first five cups of melted cider
will be strong enough to use as
concentrate.

MAKES ONE 9-INCH PIE.

Sugarless Muffins

Jane Ammerman
Eugene, Oregon

1 egg

⅓ cup oil

1 ripe banana, cut up

1⅓ cups unbleached flour

½ cup oatmeal, bran, or whole wheat flour

2 teaspoons baking powder

½ teaspoon salt

½ to 1½ teaspoons each of cloves, cinnamon, or nutmeg, or any combination thereof

2 oranges, slightly blended or
1 grated apple or applesauce or
1 cup cooked pumpkin or squash
or *1 cup cranberries or blueberries*

Water or fruit juice (if needed)

1 cup raisins (optional)

Preheat oven to 350°F. Blend egg, oil, and banana until smooth; pour into large bowl. In another bowl, mix together flours, baking powder, salt, and spices. Add to large bowl, along with fruit and berries. Add more liquid if needed and raisins (if used). Pour into greased muffin pan and bake about 20 minutes.

MAKES 12 MUFFINS.

Canned Tomatoes

. . . .

Fay Trout
Memphis, Tennessee

I thought you might be interested in the way I can tomatoes. Lots of tomatoes, usually seven to twelve years between cannings, as my canned tomatoes stay in perfect condition for many years. I have a few jars canned 16 years ago.

Choose the best of the last good ripe tomatoes, wash them, place them stem end down in a large plastic tub, and scald with very hot water. When skins start to slip, remove from hot water and place in cold water. Drain, remove skins (my almost grown, only daughter has been removing most of the skins since age 10), and core. Stab each one in the blossom end and squeeze to remove most seeds and juice. We drink lots and lots for fresh juice and still throw out a lot of "thin" juice. Put the prepared tomatoes in two 16-quart stainless steel cooking pots, cover, and place on low heat. Turn up heat as juice gathers in bottom of pots. When you have lots of juice, turn heat to high and boil until cooked.

Pour cooked tomatoes into hot sterilized jars (sterilize in the oven at 225°F) and seal with sterilized caps and rings. Place in the still-hot oven until jars show bubbles going from bottom to top. Turn off oven and leave jars to cool undisturbed. If you must move the jars, do it carefully and then place on a countertop padded with thick layers of newspapers. Cover with heavy bath towels.

My canned tomatoes have nothing added, not even salt. My mother-in-law can't believe it, but she loves my canned tomatoes. My own mother never heard of not adding anything to canned tomatoes to keep them from spoiling. She, too, loved my canned tomatoes, but she's gone now. I lost her five months after I gave her 40 quarts in 1984.

When anyone opens a jar of my tomatoes, they get one quart of tomatoes, not a half quart and the rest juice.

Dilly Beans

· ·

Carolyn Stancik
Lynnwood, Washington

2 cups vinegar (at least 4 percent)

2 cups water

¼ cup salt

Fresh dill weed

Garlic

Raw green beans

Small red peppers

Bring vinegar, water, and salt to a boil. Keep hot on stove. In each canning jar put some dill, garlic, raw green beans, and a small red pepper. Process in hot water bath: 10 to 15 minutes for half-pints and pints, 20 minutes for quarts. Begin timing when water comes back to a boil.

MAKES 3 OR 4 PINTS.

Easy-Freeze Zucchini

· ·

Hulda Zahler
Milwaukie, Oregon

Just pick, wash, trim blossom and stem ends, shred, fill into containers, and freeze. (No blanching needed.) Very good for winter use in soups, casseroles, zucchini bread, etc.

Green Tomato Jam

Jennifer Mueller
Willamina, Oregon

When the frosts come, you always have things that will never ripen so must be used fairly soon. With the production of ripe tomatoes cut off, you are left with a quantity of "fruit" that it seems a pity to waste. This recipe is from England, and was originally in pounds. I adapted it to cups for use with pectin, as otherwise it was made the old-fashioned way, simply by boiling.

9 cups green tomatoes, chopped well ("They must be firm and sound, without a trace of color," says the original recipe)

6 cups sugar

1 package liquid pectin

Combine tomatoes and sugar, with a little water if needed to start things going. Simmer slowly for over an hour. This is necessary to soften the tomatoes and produce the flavor of the jam, and is why you have to use liquid pectin. When the tomatoes are soft, add the liquid pectin and follow the directions on the package.

If you want to do it the old-fashioned way, substitute pounds for cups in the proportions and omit the pectin. Just boil until you get a jelly test. That takes something like two hours. It also takes a sizable kettle.

The original says you needn't add anything like lemon peel or cinnamon for extra flavor, and I can attest it is correct. Excellent with toast or English muffins. I don't know about peanut butter.

MAKES 7 TO 9 GLASSES.

Hot or Chilled Cucumber Soup

Sieglinde Thatcher
Corvallis, Oregon

In Germany we love those overgrown, yellowed huge cucumbers. We just peel, deseed, and slice them in half lengthwise. Then we stuff them with a special ground beef mixture, secure them with a string, and brown them in bacon drippings. To this we add the strained cucumber juice (saving a little aside as an astringent for our faces), add sugar, salt, and vinegar to taste, and serve with boiled or parsleyed potatoes. But because I was given over 10 of those large cucumbers I needed a quick approach toward their preparation. I made soup. What else could I do?

About 7 handfuls peeled, seeded, and chopped cucumber

½ cup cucumber liquid (strain and stir the seeded juice through a sieve)

1½ capfuls bottled lemon juice or equivalent fresh

3 packs sugar substitute or 1½ to 2 tablespoons honey (clover honey is best)

1 tablespoon onion powder (NOT onion salt) or 3 medium-to-large onions, chopped fine and sautéed

2 teaspoons or more dried or fresh mint leaves

2 teaspoons dried or fresh dill weed

Salt and pepper to taste (easy on the pepper)

Combine all ingredients in a large pot. (I never measure exactly. When the pot is full enough, I stop.) Bring to a boil and simmer 20 minutes, stirring frequently. Taste to see if it has enough salt, etc. Liquefy in blender and pour into freezer bags. Cool to room temperature and then refrigerate. Can be served cold, reheated, or frozen for later use. (Chilling first in the refrigerator before freezing keeps ice buildup to a minimum.)

MAKES ABOUT 1 QUART.

My Mother's Frozen Tomato Recipe

Judy Rice
Middlesex, New York

1 pound hamburger

1 green pepper, chopped (optional)

1 big onion or 2 small onions

30 tomatoes

½ teaspoon oregano or less, to taste

Salt and pepper

Crumble hamburger and brown it. Add onion and green pepper (if used) as hamburger is browning. Remove from heat and cool. Dip tomatoes in boiling water a minute or two, remove from heat, and peel. Cook tomatoes in large saucepan until sloppy. Add hamburger mixture, oregano, and salt and pepper to taste. After this is mixed up and cool, put in containers and freeze. This is good over macaroni, spaghetti, or rice, and we love it over bread.

SERVES 4.

In the north, tomatoes are very susceptible to a disease called late blight. Mine get it in the first hard rain after Labor Day. The vines and the fruit develop brown spots, which spread rapidly. There is no cure, so cut your losses and destroy the plants right away. Green tomatoes with these spots won't ripen, so don't bother trying.

No-Cook Freezer Pickles

MaryAnn McDaniel
Port Angeles, Washington

1 pinch alum

4 cups white vinegar

¼ cup pickling salt

6 cups white sugar

3 quarts sliced cucumbers

1 bunch celery, cut on the diagonal

1 red sweet pepper

1½ pounds onions, sliced

Cauliflower and other vegetables
(optional)

Dissolve alum in vinegar and mix in salt and sugar. Pour over vegetables, cover, and let stand overnight. Put in containers and put in freezer. Don't eat for 4 to 6 weeks. Very crisp and good.

MAKES ABOUT 4 QUARTS.

Frozen Corn

June Owens
Riddle, Oregon

I got this recipe from a lady that used to live in Kansas. It was published in an Iowan farm paper. We like it so well that I have given up canning corn in a pressure cooker.

15 cups raw corn, cut off cob.
    Do not blanch corn.

¼ cup salt

¾ cup sugar

5 cups water

Stir everything together and place loosely in sterilized jars. Place lids and rings on and tighten. Leave 1-inch headspace for expansion or your jars will break. Freeze.

MAKES 5 QUARTS.

Okra, Green Tomato, or Sunchoke Pickles

J.P. Frances
Mustang, Oklahoma

Fresh okra, green tomatoes, or sun-
chokes (Jerusalem artichokes)

1 clove garlic per jar

1 small, fresh hot pepper per jar

½ teaspoon dill seed per jar

½ teaspoon mustard seed per jar

1 quart water

2 cups vinegar (5 percent)

⅓ cup pickling salt

Select small, unblemished vegetables and wash well. Pack into hot
sterilized jars, leaving ½-inch headspace. Add garlic, hot pepper, dill
seed, and mustard seed to each jar.

Combine water, vinegar, and
pickling salt in saucepan and bring
to a boil. (Use distilled water if tap
water is hard or has a bad taste.)
Pour over vegetables, leaving ½-
inch headspace. Wipe jar rims;
cover with metal lids and screw on
bands. Process in boiling water
bath 15 minutes.

MAKES 6 OR 7 PINTS.

Oregon Trail Sweet Dill Pickles

· ·

Iola Garrett
Azalea, Oregon

This recipe was brought to Oregon on a covered wagon by long-distant relatives. They came from Missouri over the Oregon Trail and it has been kept in the family and handed down from one generation to another. I was given the recipe in 1976 and it was then about 120 years old. It's a really good sweet dill pickle recipe and I hope somebody else can enjoy it.

Small to medium cucumbers

2 or 3 grape leaves

2 or 3 slices onion

1 clove garlic

Pinch of alum

1 bunch dill weed

¼ teaspoon pickling spice

SYRUP

1 quart vinegar

1 quart water

¼ cup pickling salt

1½ cups sugar

Soak cucumbers overnight in cold water (ice water if possible). Drain and cut into chunks or leave whole. Put grape leaves in bottom of jar and pack cukes with onion, garlic, alum, dill, and pickling spice. Bring syrup to a boil, let cool slightly, and pour over pickles. Seal at once, turn upside down, and let sit. If they don't seal they can be put into a waterbath canner, bringing water to a boil, but do not continue to boil pickles or they will get soft.

MAKES ABOUT 2 QUARTS.

Pickled Beets

....

June Owens
Riddle, Oregon

This is an old recipe and is a little bit on the sour side, so you could add more sugar. The beets seem to reach their best flavor after they have been canned about three years. That's why I make new ones every year and label them.

4 quarts small beets

3 cups vinegar

2 cups water

2½ cups sugar

1 teaspoon salt

2 teaspoons allspice

2 teaspoons whole cloves

3 inches stick cinnamon, crumbled

1 tablespoon red food coloring

Cook fresh garden beets until tender. Plunge into cold water and slip off skins. Slice, quarter, or leave whole.

Combine vinegar, water, sugar, salt, and spices. Bring to a boil and simmer 15 minutes. Add beets and simmer 5 minutes. Add red food coloring. Pack into hot sterilized jars and seal.

MAKES ABOUT 4 QUARTS.

Refer Pickles

· ·

Lena LeMoine
Lacey, Washington

2 quarts cucumbers or zucchini,
  chopped

3 medium onions, chopped

1 green pepper, chopped

¼ cup salt

4 cups vinegar

4 cups sugar

1 teaspoon turmeric

1 teaspoon celery seed

1 teaspoon mustard seed

Prepare cucumbers or zucchini and onions in tray or pan. Add salt. Cover with ice cubes and set aside for 3 hours. Drain. Heat to a boil the vinegar, sugar, turmeric, celery seed, and mustard seed. Cover vegetables with syrup and refrigerate at least 5 days before eating. Keeps for months under refrigeration.

MAKES ABOUT 3 QUARTS.

Sweet Basil Jelly

· ·

Margaret Abplanalp
Portland, Oregon

6½ cups sugar

1 cup white vinegar

1 cup lightly packed basil leaves

6 drops green food coloring

2 cups water

1 package (6 ounces) liquid pectin

Combine sugar, vinegar, basil, and food coloring. Add water and bring to a boil. Add pectin. Return to rolling boil and boil hard, uncovered, for 2 minutes, stirring constantly. Remove from heat. Carefully remove basil. Skim well.

MAKES 7 HALF-PINTS.

Sweet Cherry Freezer Jam

Victoria Persons
Seattle, Washington

1 quart ripe sweet cherries

1 quart sugar

¼ cup lemon juice

1 package (6 ounces) liquid pectin

Pit cherries and then grind or chop fine. Measure 1¾ to 2 cups fruit and juice into large pan. Mix sugar into fruit. Mix lemon juice and pectin in small bowl and stir into fruit. Stir for 2 or 3 minutes, until sugar crystals dissolve. Heat quickly to a boil and then cool. Ladle into freezer containers and freeze. (Will keep 2 or 3 weeks in refrigerator, but do not try to can.) If jam is thin, let set in containers at room temperature for 24 hours, then freeze or chill.

MAKES 4 PINTS.

Sweet Gherkins

Mrs. F.W. Robinson
Port Angeles, Washington

5 quarts (7 pounds) small cucumbers, 1½ to 3 inches long

½ cup pickling salt

1½ quarts vinegar

8 cups sugar

¾ teaspoon turmeric

2 teaspoons celery seed

2 teaspoons whole mixed pickling spices

8 one-inch pieces cinnamon stick

½ teaspoon fennel (optional)

2 teaspoons vanilla (optional)

First day - Morning: Wash cucumbers thoroughly; scrub with vegetable brush. Stem ends may be left on. Drain cucumbers, place in large crock, and cover with boiling water. Afternoon (6 to 8 hours later): Drain. Cover with fresh boiling water.

Second day - Morning: Drain, cover with fresh boiling water. Afternoon: Drain, add salt, cover with fresh boiling water.

Third day - Morning: Drain, prick cucumbers in several places with table fork. Make syrup of 3 cups vinegar and 3 cups sugar. Add turmeric, celery seed, pickling spices, cinnamon, and fennel (if used). Heat to a boil and pour over cucumbers (cucumbers will be partially covered at this point). Afternoon: Drain syrup into a saucepan. Add 2 cups sugar and 2 cups vinegar, heat to a boil, and pour back over pickles.

Fourth day - Morning: Drain syrup into saucepan, add 2 cups sugar and 1 cup vinegar, heat to a boil and pour over cucumbers. Afternoon: Drain syrup and add remaining 1 cup sugar and vanilla (if used). Heat to a boil. Pack pickles into clean hot jars and cover with the boiling syrup to ½-inch from top of jar. Adjust jar lids.

Process for 5 minutes in boiling water. (Start to count processing time as soon as water returns to a boil.) Set jars upright on wire rack.

I have never used the vanilla or fennel but everyone raves about the pickles. Real crisp.

MAKES ABOUT 5 QUARTS.

Sweet Pickles

······································

Alice Boyet
Crescent City, California

Blue ribbon winner many times.

Cucumbers

1½ cups pickling salt

1 tablespoon alum

2 quarts sugar

1 quart vinegar

3 sticks cinnamon

1 teaspoon pickling spice

Soak cucumbers in brine of salt and 4 quarts water for two weeks. Drain and wash. Slice into ½-inch slices. Dissolve alum in 2 quarts water and soak cucumbers overnight. Drain. Make hot syrup of sugar, vinegar, cinnamon, and pickling spice. Cover cucumbers with hot syrup and soak for one day. Drain cucumbers the next day, heat the syrup to boiling, and pour back over. Drain cucumbers on the third day, pack pickles in jars, and heat syrup back to a boil. Pour hot syrup over pickles and seal.

Cucumber and tomato greenhouse growers have had good results from playing classical music to their plants.

Tomato Sauce

Michael McSwiggen
Portland, Oregon

This is not really a recipe, more of a process.

We grow a lot of tomatoes, both for fresh eating and for canning. Even though the tomatoes we use for canning are the sauce variety, they have an awful lot of water to cook out. We used to run them through a food mill and then cook them down for hours. The results were not very satisfactory. Besides taking a lot of work, it takes an enormous amount of energy to evaporate a quart of water, and the sauce would often become caramelized. Since then we have found a much better way.

Clean the tomatoes, remove the stems, and cut out any bad spots. Place them in a steamer in a large (preferably stainless) pot with a half cup of water in the bottom. Start heating very slowly. As the tomatoes give up some liquid you can turn up the heat. After about half an hour, the tomato skins will start to split. Remove the pot from the heat and let it cool until you can remove the strainer. Dump the tomatoes into a colander to drain. Reserve some of the liquid in the pot for the next batch. Let the tomatoes in the colander drain until they are cool enough to handle. Blend them in a blender or food processor and can (we use a pressure cooker because it is faster, safer, and uses less energy). The liquid that has drained off is quite clear with a yellow/red tinge. We can it as well. It makes a great soup broth for light vegetable soups.

If the steaming was done at a low enough temperature and the broth was not reheated, it sometimes jells. I think that it may be a natural pectin in the tomatoes that is denatured with enough heat. Some more adventurous than I might be able to find a use for this.

The yield is about 50-50, one quart liquid for each quart purée.

Editor's Note: I tried this and it works. The liquid is also delicious to drink chilled with a little lemon pepper mix or other savory seasoning. I run the steamed tomatoes through a food mill instead of blending them because I don't like little bits of peel in my sauce.

Green Tomato Mincemeat

....

Jennifer Mueller
Willamina, Oregon

You may have a humongous lot of green tomatoes, as my nephew says. Or only a few. Or a lot of half-ripe split ones you can't use for jam. So you make green tomato mincemeat. Make it to taste. The proportions given here are pretty elastic.

For every 2 cups of green tomatoes, chopped small, you want:

1½ to 2½ cups of apples, cored, pared, and chopped (depending on your apple supply)

½ to 1 cup raisins (depending on price and how much you like them)

1 large carrot, grated

1 to 1½ cups sugar (depending on taste preference, sweetness of apples, and quantity of raisins)

¼ cup molasses

½ to 1 cup cider, orange juice, or water, if it needs more liquid

At least 1 teaspoon cinnamon or apple pie spice

½ teaspoon salt

The recipe I adapted this from called for ½ cup grated suet, hard to find and possibly not wanted in these days of cholesterol consciousness. But some richness is desirable; I would say substitute about 3 tablespoons margarine.

You can always make it a real mincemeat by adding hamburger —coarsely ground if you can get it—between 1 and 2 cups. Omit other shortening in that case.

Boil it all together to give the flavors time to blend, and taste to see if it does need more sugar or spice before bottling. You may can it in the usual way. However, you may not have a canning kettle or may not want to bother with one, in which case you can wash your jars and fill them with hot water. Have small pan of water boiling. Take each jar, empty the water, and fill with boiling mincemeat. Use a canning funnel to keep the rim clean. Scald your lid—let it stay a little longer than usual—then slap it on the jar and screw a ring down on it until your eyes pop. Repeat with the next jar, and so on, doing one at a time. Most if not all will seal.

If you don't have canning jars, this can be preserved like jam, with melted paraffin wax poured over it. Remember, the original reason for mincemeat was preservative—the sugar and spices kept the meat from spoiling, so you don't have to worry about food poisoning.

If you don't eat mince pies yourself, I find they go very well at bake sales.

Finnish Pickled Cucumbers

Liisa Prehn
Kirkland, Washington

About 50 small pickling cucumbers

Washed leaves of black currant

¼ pound horseradish, minced (optional)

2 to 4 cloves garlic, crushed

1 tablespoon whole white peppers

BRINE

5 quarts water

2 cups kosher salt (rough salt)

1 cup white distilled vinegar

Layer the washed cucumbers with black currant leaves (1 or 2 leaves per layer) and spices in a large glass jar. Bring brine to a boil and pour carefully over the pickles. Refrigerate when cooled. Ready to eat in about 6 weeks.

MAKES ABOUT 1 GALLON.

Cucumbers need a constant supply of water or the fruits will be bitter. You can sink a flower pot into the ground near the plant and fill it periodically.

Rhubarb Relish

··

Marshall A. Voight
Ferndale, Washington

Serve with cold meats, hot dogs, fish, baked beans, etc. Delicious.

1 quart finely chopped rhubarb

1 quart chopped onion

3½ cups sugar

¾ cup water

1 teaspoon salt

1 teaspoon cinnamon

1 teaspoon allspice

1 teaspoon cloves

Combine ingredients in a large stainless steel or enamel kettle. Do not use aluminum or cast iron. Bring to a boil. Reduce heat and simmer about an hour, stirring occasionally. Fill sterilized jars and process 10 to 15 minutes in water bath.

MAKES ABOUT 3 PINTS.

Zucchini Relish

....

Carolyn Stancik
Lynnwood, Washington

10 cups chopped zucchini

4 cups chopped onions

1 green pepper

1 red pepper

5 tablespoons salt

4 cups sugar

2½ cups cider vinegar

1 teaspoon mustard seed

1 teaspoon turmeric

½ teaspoon cloves

½ teaspoon allspice

½ teaspoon pepper

1 teaspoon celery seed

1 tablespoon cornstarch

Grind together the zucchini, onion, and peppers. Add salt and let stand overnight. The next day, drain the mixture and add remaining ingredients. Mix well and cook 35 minutes. Seal in sterilized jars while hot. Or cook in filled canning jars in open water method.

MAKES 5 OR 6 PINTS.

Canned Salsa

· ·

Greg Oline
Rickrall, Oregon

5 pounds tomatoes (about 15 tomatoes), peeled and chopped

1 pound onion (3 medium onions),
chopped

6 or 7 fresh jalapeño peppers,
chopped

2 green peppers, chopped

3 stalks celery, chopped

3 teaspoons salt

¾ cup vinegar

1½ teaspoons cumin

9 dried chile peppers, crushed

1 teaspoon garlic powder

½ teaspoon pepper

Mix together and bring to a boil.
Simmer 10 minutes. Put into clean
hot jars and process 15 minutes by
hot pack method.

MAKES ABOUT 7 PINTS.

Winter

A Lentil Soup Recipe for the Health-Conscious Ones

Jan Davis
Calistoga, California

Apple juice

3 or 4 bunches green onions, including green parts

1 large red onion, chopped

1 whole bunch celery, chopped

1 Savoy cabbage, chopped

1 bunch spinach, chopped

4 or 5 cups dried lentils

2 or 3 pounds mushrooms, chopped (more if you like mushrooms)

¼ cup mixed fresh herbs: rosemary, thyme, sage, oregano, and basil or ¼ ounce dried Italian herb mix

Sauté green and red onions in a small amount of apple juice over low heat. Add celery, Savoy cabbage, spinach, lentils, mushrooms, and herbs. If you use enough herbs, you won't have to add salt to make it tasty. Add water to make 10 to 12 quarts of soup. Simmer on low all day or until thick enough and package most of the soup for the freezer.

MAKES 10 OR 12 QUARTS.

If you have trouble raising cabbage-family plants and you don't have poor soil or rootfly maggot, your problem may be clubroot, a soilborne fungus that can stay dormant up to seven years. My clubroot problems diminished markedly when I began liming my soil more conscientiously. Four-year (minimum) crop rotation also helps. That includes cruciferous weeds like shepherd's purse. One folk remedy is to put a piece of rhubarb stalk down each hole where you transplant a cole crop.

Cream of Winter Vegetable Soup

....

Phyllis Michelson
Ridgefield, Washington

2 cups chopped peeled potatoes

1½ cups chopped peeled winter
    squash

½ cup celery

1 small onion, chopped

1 clove garlic, minced

2 tablespoons snipped parsley

1 teaspoon dry mustard

1 teaspoon grated lemon peel

⅛ teaspoon pepper

1 can (10¾ ounces) chicken broth or
    1 or 2 chicken bouillon cubes

1¼ cups milk

Sunflower seeds or chopped nuts

Combine all but the stock and milk in a large pan. Stir in stock and bring to boil. Reduce heat, cover, and simmer 20 minutes or until vegetables are tender. Remove 2 cups of mixture and purée in blender or food processor. Return purée to saucepan, stir in milk, and heat through. Season to taste. Sprinkle sunflower seeds or nuts over each serving.

SERVES 6 OR 8.

Curried Pumpkin Soup

Margot Becker
Snohomish, Washington

This soup was originally in *Bon Appetit.* I took the calories out.

1 teaspoon dried onion

1 teaspoon curry powder

¾ cup pumpkin or squash purée

1 cup chicken broth

1 tablespoon brown sugar

Dash hot-pepper sauce

Pepper

Nutmeg

1 cup milk (whole or skim)

Plain low-fat yogurt

Chives

Place onion and curry in pot. Add pumpkin, chicken broth, and seasonings. Bring to boil. Simmer 5 minutes. Add milk and cook until hot (do not boil). Serve with garnish of yogurt and chives.

SERVES 2 OR 3.

Scarlet Emperor Bean Soup

Sylvia Goheen
Olympia, Washington

This bean I think makes the best soup. Its flavor is wonderful. I only grow it in order to dry the beans. The best method is to plan for two days so you can skim off the hardened fat. It also can be made as a vegetarian soup. Increase beans to 2 cups; add salt for flavor. This can be done in one day since no meat fat is involved. With cornbread it makes for a very comfort-inducing meal.

3 quarts water

1½ pounds smoked ham hocks

1½ cups dried scarlet emperor beans

2 bay leaves

⅛ teaspoon pepper

1 cup chopped onions, divided

⅛ to ¼ teaspoon chili powder (more if you like hot)

2 cloves garlic, minced

1 cup chopped celery

About 5 large ripe tomatoes, cut into quarters, or a large can whole tomatoes with juice

Bring hocks to boil in large soup pot with 3 quarts water. Simmer 1½ to 2 hours, until hocks are very tender. Remove. When cool, break up hocks in bite-sized pieces, discarding fat and skin (unless you're feeling sinful and happen to like the skin, as we do!). Refrigerate ham and cool soup overnight in the refrigerator. The next day, skim off hard fat.

Add beans, bay leaves, pepper, ½ cup onions, chili powder, and garlic. Bring to a boil and simmer 1 hour or until beans are almost tender, adding a little more water if necessary. Add rest of onions, celery, and tomatoes and cook another 45 minutes to 1 hour. Put in reserved ham and serve with corn bread or a crusty sourdough loaf. For those of us who really appreciate onions and don't have any important social engagements, sprinkle a couple tablespoons finely chopped onions on the soup in the bowl before eating.

IT FEEDS A LOT—WHO CAN MAKE SOUP FOR TWO?

Vegetable (No-Fat) Soup

George W. Mengelkoch
Portland, Oregon

Japanese eat this soup with chopsticks. They pick out the vegetables with chopsticks then drink the liquid from the bowl.

1 or 2 cups boiling water

Any available vegetables such as cabbage, lettuce, radishes, roots, celery, carrots, all chopped

Soy sauce to taste

Add vegetables to boiling water. Cook to crisp-tender. Add soy sauce to taste.

SERVES 1 OR 2.

Carrot Salad

Diana Anderson
Enumclaw, Washington

1 clove garlic, minced

⅛ teaspoon pepper

1 tablespoon lemon juice

2 tablespoons oil

3 tablespoons minced parsley

3 large carrots, coarsely shredded

Combine dressing ingredients. Add parsley and carrots. Mix well.

SERVES 4.

Carrot-Lemon Salad

···

Diana Anderson
Enumclaw, Washington

¼ cup water

¼ cup sugar

3 tablespoons lemon juice

2 teaspoons grated lemon rind

3 cups grated carrots

Boil sugar and water to dissolve sugar. Cool. Combine all ingredients. This is very good over cottage cheese.

SERVES 3 OR 4.

Glorified Cabbage Salad

···

June Hadland
Chehalis, Washington

My own creation; loved by all.

2 or 3 cups cabbage

1 cup pineapple, fresh, canned, or dry

6 to 12 dates, cut fine

½ cup raisins

1½ bananas

2 small red apples

1¼ cups chopped filberts, walnuts, or cashews

⅓ cup mayonnaise or salad dressing, thinned with pineapple juice

Mix together and refrigerate before serving.

SERVES 3 OR 4.

Green Green Slaw

· ·

Barbara Rozelle
Seattle, Washington

4 cups shredded cabbage

¾ cup sliced celery

¾ to 1 cup seedless green grapes

¾ cup undrained crushed pineapple

½ cup low-cholesterol mayonnaise

2 tablespoons honey

Nutmeg

Mix well. Season with nutmeg.
Keeps well.

SERVES 6.

Jicama-Carrot Salad

· ·

Jan Brown
Clinton, Washington

1 cup grated jicama root

2 cups grated carrot

*¼ cup chopped green onion, includ-
ing tops*

¼ cup chopped parsley

¼ cup sunflower seeds

Combine salad ingredients in bowl
and toss with vinegar and oil dressing (cider vinegar is the best with
olive oil).

SERVES 4.

Kale Salad

·······························

Valerie Perry
Keizer, Oregon

In the winter when lettuce is limp or too expensive to buy, we eat kale salad a lot. First we de-stem kale leaves and chop them to mouth-sized pieces, then steam for 20 minutes or so. If we're in a hurry, we use our pressure cooker brought up to pressure for 2 or 3 minutes and quickly cooled under running water. Mix cooked kale with other vegetables and toss with your fav-orite salad dressing. This is delicious, hot or cold. No grown person has ever disliked kale prepared like this. Some small people have also been known to eat reasonable quantities. The salad is especially tasty and attractive with raw red pepper or cooked carrots. Be sure to make a lot—it keeps well in the refrigerator for a quick salad meal.

Roberto's Sweet Cabbage

·······························

Bob Brooks
Seattle, Washington

Ketjap manis is Indonesian sweet soy sauce, sweetened with palm sugar. Regular soy sauce and brown sugar can be substituted.

Sesame oil

Ginger, chopped fine

Garlic, chopped fine

Cabbage (any variety), cut in 1-inch chunks

Dry sherry

Ketjap manis

Cornstarch

Fry ginger and garlic in small amount of sesame oil. Add cabbage chunks and fry over high heat, separating into single layers. Add sherry and ketjap manis and a little water. Cover and cook until tender. Thicken with cornstarch dissolved in a little cold water.

Red Cabbage Salad

Caroline Robinson
Everett, Washington

This salad is one of those that gets a strange look. The first bite gets chewed slowly, but then the rest of them just seem to go in faster and faster. This salad is very crunchy, sweet, and addictive. Oh, and terribly healthy.

1 medium head red cabbage, chopped into bite-sized pieces

10 radishes, sliced (I like slices to be sliced again in half)

2 or 3 Granny Smith or other tart apples, diced

2 stalks green onion, chopped

Celery, chopped (optional)

Walnuts, chopped (optional)

1 or 2 tablespoons fresh lemon juice

Dash garlic salt

2 or 3 tablespoons zesty Italian dressing

Mix everything in a bowl and let sit for an hour, stirring once or twice.

SERVES 4 TO 6.

Red Cabbage Slaw

Mildred Stephenson
Half Moon Bay, California

1 large head red cabbage, sliced thin

1 large sweet onion, in rings

1 cup plus 1 tablespoon sugar

1 cup vinegar

½ cup salad oil

1 teaspoon celery seed

1 tablespoon salt

Sprinkle 1 cup sugar between alternate layers of thinly sliced cabbage and onions. End with layer of onions. Combine vinegar, remaining tablespoon sugar, salad oil, celery seed, and salt in a saucepan, bring to a boil, and pour over cabbage and onions. Marinate overnight.

Winter Salad

∙∙∙

Freida Fenn
Port Townsend, Washington

Original recipe.

⅓ cup olive oil

⅓ cup balsamic vinegar

1 tablespoon dried basil

2 teaspoons dried tarragon

½ teaspoon dried oregano

¼ cup tamari soy sauce

Dash cayenne pepper

*1 pound firm tofu, drained and
cubed*

1 small red cabbage, shredded

*1 bunch mizuna (mild mustard
greens), chopped*

⅔ cup chopped parsley

2 red bell peppers, slivered

1 can black olives, drained and sliced

⅔ cup cashews, toasted

½ pound feta cheese, crumbled

Mix together vinegar, basil, tarragon, oregano, tamari, and cayenne. Add tofu and marinate while you prepare rest of salad. Mix remaining ingredients into marinated tofu. Toss well and serve. Keeps well if prepared a day ahead.

Editor's Note: Tamari has a lower salt content and more subtle flavor than standard soy sauce. You may want to reduce the amount if you are using another type.

SERVES 12.

Winter Gold Carrot Salad

Mrs. John W. Huff
Puyallup, Washington

5 cups sliced carrots

1 green pepper, thinly sliced

1 medium onion, thinly sliced

1 cup thinly sliced celery

1 cup sliced water chestnuts

1 can (10 ounces) tomato soup

½ cup vegetable oil

¾ cup sugar

¾ cup vinegar

½ teaspoon pepper

1 tablespoon prepared mustard

1 tablespoon salt

1 tablespoon Worcestershire sauce

Steam carrots until crisp-tender. Cool. Place in large bowl with green pepper, onion, celery, and water chestnuts.

Combine remaining ingredients and mix well. Pour half the marinade over vegetables and refrigerate overnight. Save remaining marinade for lettuce. Salad will keep well for two weeks in refrigerator.

SERVES 8.

Treat carrot rows gently. Rough thinning and hoeing can damage the roots, and the smell of a bruised carrot attracts hordes of carrot flies, whose voracious larvae can decimate a winter crop. You can minimize disturbance by thinning and weeding in the rain and firming the soil afterwards.

Witloof (Belgian Chicory) the Antwerp Way

Rosa Chapman
Wildwood, California

4 to 6 heads Witloof chicory

4 to 6 slices Danish or other finely
sliced ham

¼ cup grated mixed Romano and
Parmesan cheese

¼ cup grated Swiss cheese

6 or 7 cooked potatoes

Butter or margarine

Milk to taste

Preheat oven to 375°F. Blanch chicory and wash briefly under cold running water. With a sharp knife, cut a small sliver off bottom of each rosette and remove inner core. This will decrease the bitter taste which sometimes detracts from the dish.

Cook rosettes for a few minutes in boiling water. Do not overcook. They should be firm but done. Drain. Remove fat from ham. Wrap each rosette in a slice of ham and place in the bottom of a lightly greased ovenproof casserole dish. Top with grated cheese.

Mash potatoes with butter or margarine and milk and spread over Witloof and cheese, leaving some peaks. Cover casserole and bake 15 to 20 minutes. Remove cover and brown slightly under the grill.

Editor's Note: Witloof is the pale, pricy vegetable served in French restaurants as endive.

SERVES 4.

Beef Stew by Kay

Kay Holland
Poulsbo, Washington

I guarantee this is the best-tasting stew you will ever eat. It is further enhanced with a side of steamed artichokes and a glass of chilled rosé wine.

¼ cup flour

1 teaspoon salt

¼ teaspoon freshly ground pepper

2 pounds beef stew meat

2 tablespoons olive oil

2 medium onions, sliced

1 clove garlic, minced

2 cups water or 1 cup water and 1
    cup dry red wine

⅔ cup (4-ounce can) undrained
    mushrooms

1 cube or 1 teaspoon beef bouillon

1 stick cinnamon

1 bay leaf

2 cups sliced celery

3 cups sliced carrots

1 tablespoon chopped parsley

Combine flour, salt, and pepper. Coat meat pieces with flour mixture. In Dutch oven, brown meat, onion slices, and garlic in hot oil. Reduce heat and add water, wine (if used), mushrooms, bouillon, cinnamon, and bay leaf. Simmer, covered, for 2 hours. Remove cinnamon stick and bay leaf. Add celery, carrots, and parsley; simmer until vegetables are tender but not mushy. Serve over baked potatoes.

SERVES 6 TO 8.

Bierrocks

··

Susan Stapoulos
Tacoma, Washington

These meat-filled buns are great for a picnic or for a casual "supper in hand" served with cold veggies. A good way to use cabbage.

DOUGH

2 packages dry yeast

2 cups warm water

¼ cup sugar

1½ teaspoons salt

1 egg, beaten

¼ cup melted margarine

6 to 6½ cups flour

FILLING

1½ pounds ground beef

½ cup onion

3 cups finely cut cabbage

1½ teaspoons salt

½ teaspoon pepper

1 tablespoon Worcestershire sauce or
  dash hot-pepper sauce

Dissolve yeast in water. Add sugar, salt, egg, margarine, and flour. Knead until smooth and elastic. Chill dough several hours.

Brown beef and onion in skillet. Add cabbage, salt, pepper, and Worcestershire or hot-pepper sauce. Cover skillet and continue cooking over low heat, stirring occasionally, until cabbage is tender. Do not add liquid. Cool slightly.

Remove dough from refrigerator. Pinch off a handful of dough (about the size of a golf ball) and roll it into a circle about ⅛-inch thick (about 5 inches in diameter). Place 2 tablespoons of meat mixture in center and pinch edges together, and place pinched-side-down on greased cookie sheet. Repeat process till dough and meat are used up. Preheat oven to 350°F and let pastries rise 15 minutes. Bake for 20 to 30 minutes.

SERVES 10.

Boerenkool
Kale and potatoes

· ·

Aaron Flier
Pacifica, California

A national Holland winter dish.

4 bunches of kale

6 large potatoes

1 Dutch mattwurst or Polish sausage

Strip kale leaves from stems and wash thoroughly. Boil in salt water until tender. Drain and chop fine. Add potatoes and sausage pricked with a fork. Boil slowly for about 1 hour. Remove sausages and mash potatoes and kale. Season to taste and add beef drippings or butter. Serve on platter with sausage in the middle on top of kale.

SERVES ABOUT 6.

Beet Purée

· ·

Deb Jacobson
Mercer Island, Washington

3 pounds beets

4 tablespoons butter

¼ cup cider vinegar

1 tablespoon sugar

Boil beets until tender, 1 hour or so. Rinse in cold water and peel skins. Purée in processor or food mill. Melt butter. Add vinegar and sugar. Blend with beets on low.

SERVES 6.

Borscht

Geraldeen Linnell
Vancouver, Washington

1 large beef soup bone

1 large onion, chopped

5 or 6 large beets, cooked, peeled
   and diced

½ head cabbage, chopped

2 or 3 carrots, diced

1 teaspoon fresh dill weed or dill seed

½ cup sour cream

Salt and pepper to taste

Place beef bone and chopped onion in a large stock pot with 6 to 8 quarts of water. Bring to a boil and then lower heat and simmer for 5 to 6 hours. About an hour before serving, add the cabbage, carrots, and dill. Bring to a slow boil and cook until tender. Add beets and sour cream. Serve with a slice of garlic toast.

Editor's Note: Depending on your soup bone, you may want to skim fat off the stock before adding the vegetables. Meat can be removed from the bone, shredded, and returned to soup if desired.

SERVES 8.

Cooking beets by boiling or baking takes a long time. A microwave speeds the process tremendously. Cook four beets in ¼ cup water for about 15 minutes. You can freeze the ones you don't use right away.

Buttercup Squash

· ·

Ruth Barnes
Sequim, Washington

Since in our area buttercup squash (our favorite) tends to be dry, I have found this a wonderful way to cook it. Carefully cut off stem so squash will sit level. Carve the blossom end out as you would a jack o'lantern lid. Clean out seeds.

Salt, pepper, and butter to taste and fill with boiling water. Put lid back on, set in a cake pan, and bake until done, about 1 hour, depending on size. I serve as is at the table.

Cabbage, Corn, and Tomato Sauce with Cheese and Olives

· ·

Sharon Marvin
Umpqua, Oregon

1 pint home-canned tomato sauce

Half a medium onion, sliced thin in half rings

6 cups cabbage, cut into 1-inch chunks

1 cup frozen corn

¾ cup sliced black olives

1 cup grated Cheddar or Monterey jack cheese

Cayenne pepper to taste

Put tomato sauce, onion, cabbage, and corn in a stainless steel skillet. Heat through on medium heat, stirring occasionally. The less you cook the cabbage, the better it will be for you. Just crisp-tender would be perfect. Remove from heat and stir in olives, cheese, and cayenne.

SERVES 4.

Carrot Casserole

Donna Dreessen
Port Orchard, Washington

12 carrots

¼ cup butter

¼ cup flour

2 cups milk

1 teaspoon salt

¼ teaspoon dry mustard

1 teaspoon chopped onion or dried
onion flakes

½ pound mild Cheddar cheese,
grated

3 cups buttered bread crumbs
or cubes

Cook whole carrots for 20 minutes, then cut in chunks. Make white sauce using butter, flour, and milk. When thickened, add salt, mustard, onion, celery, and cheese. Stir over low heat until cheese is melted. Put carrots in 2-quart casserole and pour cheese sauce over top. Top with buttered bread crumbs or cubes. Bake at 350°F for 30 to 40 minutes.

SERVES 8 TO 10.

Insufficient water causes radishes to become hard and woody, carrots stumpy, and lettuce bitter. Underwatered tomatoes tend to drop their blossoms.

Carrot Loaf

Nora Olson
Lorane, Oregon

1 teaspoon chopped onion

3 tablespoons melted butter

1 cup bread crumbs

2 cups raw grated carrots

2 eggs, slightly beaten

1½ cups milk

1 teaspoon salt

⅛ teaspoon pepper

Preheat oven to 350°F. Brown onion in butter and add to bread crumbs. Add other ingredients and mix well. Bake in bread pan until firm, about 30 minutes. Your favorite cheese sauce adds much to the loaf.

SERVES 6.

Hungarian Stuffed Celeriac

Ann Kosanovic-Brown
Seattle, Washington

*1½ pounds (3 or 4) even-sized
   celeriac*

1 cup (4 ounces) chopped mushrooms

¾ cup (3 ounces) grated cheese

4 tablespoons butter

¼ cup sour cream

Salt

Preheat oven to 375°F. Peel celeriacs and cook in salted water until nearly done. Drain, cool slightly, and scoop out the insides carefully. Chop celeriac scoopings fine and combine with mushrooms and grated cheese. Stuff celeriac shells with this mixture. Place in a baking dish and top each one with sour cream and butter. Bake for 30 minutes and serve hot.

SERVES 3 OR 4.

Celeriac Purée

....

Ann Kosanovic-Brown
Seattle, Washington

*1½ pounds celeriac, peeled and
   cubed*

6 tablespoons butter

Salt and pepper

1 cup vegetable stock

1 tablespoon flour

Heat butter in a saucepan and add celeriac, salt, pepper, and half the vegetable stock. Cover and simmer, stirring once or twice, until celeriac is soft and stock evaporates. Sprinkle with flour, stir, and add remaining stock. Bring to boil, lower heat, and cook 10 minutes longer. Mash with potato masher to remove any remaining lumps. Serve instead of mashed potatoes.

Editor's Note: To avoid discoloration, put the cut celeriac in acidulated water (1 tablespoon vinegar or lemon juice per quart) until cooking time.

SERVES 4.

For fresh winter mint, dig up some roots before the first freeze and grow them inside the house or in a greenhouse.

Chicken and Carrots Fricassee

··

Victoria Persons
Seattle, Washington

1 pound carrots

1 tablespoon lemon juice

1 cup chopped leeks

3 tablespoons butter

1 tablespoon flour

½ cup chicken broth

2 whole chicken breasts, halved

1 tablespoon chopped tarragon

½ cup cream or milk

Salt and pepper to taste

Peel and slice carrots into ¼-inch sticks, 2 to 3 inches long. Sprinkle with lemon juice and add leeks. Melt butter in skillet, add carrots and leeks, and sauté on medium heat for 3 to 5 minutes. Sprinkle with flour and stir to make roux. Stir in broth. Place chicken breasts on top of carrots. Cover and simmer until chicken is tender. With a slotted spoon, remove chicken and vegetables to platter and keep warm. Add cream or milk to roux, simmer to reduce slightly, and add tarragon, salt, and pepper. Pour over chicken and serve.

Editor's Note: I doubled this recipe by using more vegetables and a whole chicken, which I poached in a little white wine until it was mostly cooked. Then I took the meat off the bones and proceeded with the recipe as given. It was economical and absolutely delicious.

SERVES 4.

Cooking Sunchokes
Jerusalem artichokes

J.P. Frances
Mustang, Oklahoma

Peeling is unnecessary but do wash very well and scrub clean with brush. Remove discolored and damaged spots. May be steamed or boiled. Add 1 teaspoon vinegar to each cup of water. Cooking times: 12 to 15 minutes for whole chokes; 6 to 8 minutes for sliced. At these times, test for doneness with fork or toothpick. Do not overcook. Mash and serve with your favorite potato topping, or leave in slices or chunks as you prefer. A delicately flavored cream sauce is very acceptable, or herbed butter.

In the unlikely event that you don't have enough Jerusalem artichoke tubers for planting, they can be cut up like potatoes and each piece will produce a new plant.

Curried Carrots with Pineapple

Paula Simmons
Sardis, British Columbia

Make a big batch; it reheats well in the microwave.

1½ pounds peeled and sliced or
*   chunked carrots*

1 cup water

1 can (20 ounces) chunk pineapple

1½ tablespoons cornstarch

2 tablespoons butter or margarine

1 teaspoon curry powder, or to taste

Boil carrots in water until barely tender, drain, and reserve cooking water. Boil down cooking water to ⅓ cup. Drain pineapple chunks and reserve juice (should be about ¾ cup). Add pineapple chunks to carrots. Melt margarine in nonstick pan and stir in curry powder. Mix cornstarch into pineapple juice. Combine with carrot water and add to curry mixture. Cook slowly until thickened. Add carrots and pineapple and heat until bubbly and all heated through.

SERVES 6 TO 8.

Easy Dinner

· ·

Molly LaFayette

Good with coleslaw for unexpected company, or when you've worked too long in the garden or come home late from shopping, and everyone is starving.

1 quart canned green beans

4 large potatoes, cut in half

1 onion or 2 leeks, sliced

1 carrot, peeled and sliced

1 quart canned meat with juices or *4 cups cooked chopped meat with juices* or *1 pound cooked, drained hamburger*

¼ cup cornstarch or arrowroot

½ cup brewer's yeast

1 teaspoon vegetable seasoning or salt

I like Blue Lake or purple podded pole beans, Yellow Finn potatoes, Carumba carrots, Durabell leeks, and chicken, venison, or chevon (goat) for meat. My onions are always sick—of the few that come up—so no preference.

Drain half the juice from the beans into a Dutch oven or large skillet with lid. Add potatoes, onions or leeks, and carrots to bean juice and cook until potatoes are done, 20 to 30 minutes.

Add beans and meat to cooked potatoes and heat through. Drain the other half of the bean juice into a small bowl. Add brewer's yeast and cornstarch or arrowroot and mix with fork or wire whisk until smooth. When bean and meat mixture is hot, pour in juice and brewer's yeast mixture. Stir until thickened, about 3 to 5 minutes.

Note: I have waterless cookware, so you may want to add ½ cup water with your potatoes.

SERVES 4 (I HAVE SIX KIDS SO I ALWAYS MAKE DOUBLE).

Escarole en Casserole

Lane Morgan
Sumas, Washington

2 large heads escarole or chicory

Salt and pepper

1 tablespoon chopped parsley
(optional)

1 large clove garlic, minced

½ cup olive oil

¼ cup Parmesan cheese

Preheat oven to 425°F. Separate escarole or chicory leaves, wash thoroughly, and drain. If the outer leaves are really bitter, discard them. Roll leaves gently in a dish towel to absorb extra water. Unroll and cut crosswise into 1-inch ribbons.

Place a layer of greens in a shallow casserole, sprinkle with salt, pepper, parsley (if used), and garlic and drizzle with olive oil. Continue layering until greens are used up. Sprinkle with remaining seasonings and top with Parmesan. Bake 15 or 20 minutes. Greens should be browned on top, tender underneath.

SERVES 4.

When transplanting cabbages, dip roots in a mixture of mud and lime, or manure tea and dirt. The roots will benefit from immediate contact with nutrients.

Grandfather's Shaggy Dogs

Paula Simmons
Sardis, British Columbia

2 large baking potatoes, scrubbed
and shredded

½ cup chopped leftover meat

1 egg, beaten

1 tablespoon finely chopped onion

¼ to ½ teaspoon salt

Generous sprinkling fresh ground
pepper

¼ cup flour

½ teaspoon baking powder

2 tablespoons melted margarine

Mix potatoes with meat and stir in all but margarine. Drop by tablespoonfuls into skillet. Fry in margarine until golden brown on both sides.

Editor's Note: This recipe doesn't work with new potatoes.

SERVES 6.

Hamburger Stew

Nina Wells
Independence, Oregon

1½ pounds ground beef

2 medium onions, chopped

1½ quarts home-canned tomatoes

6 to 8 medium potatoes, diced

Salt and pepper

Brown beef and onion. Add tomatoes with their liquid, potatoes, and salt and pepper to taste. Simmer until potatoes are tender, about 1 hour. Great served with fresh hot rolls or bread and salad.

SERVES 6.

Herbed Tomato-Cheese Bread with Sour Cream Topping

Bev Miguel
Sebastopol, California

This dish may be wrapped in foil and refrigerated. It reheats beautifully. I have never tried the "variation" as I like the other so well.

2 tablespooons butter

1 medium onion, minced

¾ cup sour cream

⅓ cup mayonnaise

1 cup grated (4 ounces) grated Cheddar cheese

¾ teaspoon salt

¼ teaspoon pepper

¼ teaspoon dried (not powdered) oregano

Pinch of sage

⅔ cup milk

2 cups biscuit mix

3 medium tomatoes, peeled and sliced ¼-inch thick

Paprika

Make topping by melting butter in saucepan or small skillet. Sauté onion until tender. Remove from heat and blend in sour cream, mayonnaise, Cheddar, salt, pepper, oregano, and sage. Set aside. Butter a 9-by-13-inch baking dish. Stir milk into biscuit mix to make a soft dough. Turn dough onto well-floured board and knead lightly 10 to 12 strokes. Pat dough over bottom of baking dish, pushing up the sides to form a shallow rim. Arrange tomato slices over dough. Spoon on topping and sprinkle with paprika. Bake 20 to 25 minutes. Let stand about 10 minutes before cutting.

Variation: Reduce salt to ½ teaspoon. Omit Cheddar, oregano, and sage. Add 3 tablespoons minced pimiento, 2 tablespoons shredded Parmesan cheese, 1½ teaspoons minced parsley, and ⅛ teaspoon basil. Omit tomatoes.

SERVES 12.

Kale and Potato Stir-Fry

Mary Vincent
Seattle, Washington

This is our absolutely most favorite recipe for February. Proportions may be varied depending on taste and size of the crowd to feed.

2 tablespoons butter, oil, or
  combination

1 onion, chopped

2 or 3 potatoes, cubed

Water

1 bunch kale, chopped

Sauté onion in butter or oil in heavy skillet. Add potatoes and water. Cover and steam until potatoes are almost tender. (I often use leftover baked potatoes and omit the steaming.) Add kale. Stir-fry, and then cover and steam until tender.

SERVES 4.

Lentil Sprouts with Rice and Cottage Cheese

Sharon Marvin
Umpqua, Oregon

I really feel that since variety in the garden is somewhat limited during the winter, sprouting is an option that should be kept in mind. Here's what I find to be a particularly palatable and healthful way to serve lentil sprouts.

In a wide, shallow serving bowl, put equal portions of warm cooked brown rice with butter, sprouted lentils (½-inch long tails), and cottage cheese. The rice and lentils should be drizzled with a tiny bit of tamari or soy sauce (use according to taste but don't overdo). Sprouts and garden vegetables make you feel great!

SERVES 1.

Lemon-Baked Potatoes

Mrs. M. Shishido
Forest Grove, Oregon

⅓ cup butter or margarine

3 tablespoons lemon juice

1½ teaspoons minced garlic

¾ teaspoon dried dill weed

¼ teaspoon grated lemon peel

⅛ teaspoon hot-pepper sauce

3 large Idaho potatoes

Preheat oven to 425°F. In a small bowl combine butter or margarine, lemon juice, garlic, dill, lemon peel, and hot-pepper sauce. Mix well. Cut potatoes in half lengthwise. Make deep slits in cut surface every ¼ inch, being careful not to cut through skin. Arrange in shallow baking pan. Brush with half the butter mixture. Bake 1 hour, brushing with remaining butter mixture every 15 minutes.

SERVES 6.

Roast Roots

E. Fuller
Portland, Oregon

Preheat oven to 375°F. Lightly grease a shallow baking pan. Arrange a selection of scrubbed, trimmed roots, including beets, potatoes, sweet potatoes, leeks, onions (quartered or halved), carrots, and parsnips. Sprinkle with olive oil and roast for 1 to 1¼ hours. Carrots and beets can be halved or started roasting ½ hour before the other roots.

Serve hot, warm, or at room temperature, with green salad and bread.

NUMBER SERVED VARIES
WITH APPETITES.

Marinated Brussels Sprouts

··

Mildred Stephenson
Half Moon Bay, California

2 pounds small firm Brussels sprouts,
    cooked

1 pound fresh button mushrooms

1 bottle Italian salad dressing

¼ teaspoon dry mustard

1 tablespoon Worcestershire sauce

2 cloves garlic, mashed

Green onions, chopped

Parsley, chopped

Mix together Brussels sprouts, mushrooms, salad dressing, mustard, Worcestershire sauce, and garlic. Refrigerate overnight. The next day, add green onions and parsley to taste. I grow all but the mushrooms in my garden.

SERVES 3 TO 5.

Mashed Potatoes Au Gratin

··

Donna Nelson
Nelson Farms, Brownsville, Oregon

6 medium potatoes, peeled and cut

½ cup butter

¼ cup sour cream

1 cup shredded Cheddar cheese

¼ cup chopped green onions
    (optional)

½ teaspoon salt (optional)

Boil potatoes until soft. Drain, add butter, sour cream, and cheese immediately, and beat with electric mixer until potatoes are fluffy and cheese is melted. Garnish with green onions or parsley.

SERVES 6 TO 8.

Our Favorite Stuffed Cabbage

Victoria Persons
Seattle, Washington

1 cup cooked shell beans (black, kidney, or white), chopped

12 outer cabbage leaves, steamed just tender

1 to 1½ cups cooked brown rice

2 tablespoons chopped parsley

2 tablespoons chopped garlic chives or 1 tablespoon regular chives and 1 tablespoon minced garlic

2 medium onions, chopped

3 medium tomatoes

1 tablespoon soy sauce

½ cup Parmesan cheese, divided

¼ cup yogurt or sour cream

¼ cup tomato juice or *⅛ cup marinara sauce and ⅛ cup water* or *¼ cup chicken or beef stock*

Preheat oven to 350°F. Mix beans with rice, herbs, and onions. Chop 1 tomato and add along with soy sauce, ¼ cup Parmesan, and yogurt or sour cream. Place 2 to 4 tablespoons of mixture on each cabbage leaf, roll up, and put on bottom of casserole dish. Chop remaining tomatoes and scatter on top of cabbage rolls. Pour on tomato sauce or juice and sprinkle with remaining cheese. Cover and bake 30 minutes, adding water or tomato juice if necessary. Serve as is or add cheese sauce or tomato sauce.

SERVES 4.

A folk method to bugproof cabbage heads is to scatter dill seed so that it rests right between the cabbage leaves.

Onions in Sage Sauce

....

Victoria Persons
Seattle, Washington

½ pound pickling onions or other
small onions

2 tablespoons butter

1 tablespoon flour

½ cup chicken stock

1 tablespoon chopped sage leaves

Salt and pepper

2 tablespoons yogurt

2 tablespoons cream

Peel onions. Heat butter in saucepan and brown onions gently, about 5 minutes. Blend in flour until smooth, and then add stock, sage, salt, and pepper to taste. Stir until smooth. Cover pan and cook 15 to 20 minutes, stirring occasionally. When onions are tender, whisk in yogurt and cream. This is especially good with roast duck or turkey.

SERVES 4 TO 6.

Onions grown from sets need special attention if you expect to save them for winter use. First, cure them at least three days in the sun before bringing them in. Also, rip off the "set" portion before drying. Onions grown from sets have two parts. One is small and extends up into a stiff hollow stem. That is the part you should rip off.

Papas a la Huancaina
Peruvian Potato Salad

....

Bárbara y Amando
Olympia, Washington

6 to 8 medium potatoes, scrubbed or
  peeled (Yellow Finns are great for
  this)

1 cup cottage cheese

1½ teaspoons ground cumin

½ to 1 teaspoon salt

⅓ cup grated raw goat cheese
  (optional)

Lettuce leaves (loose-leaf type),
  enough to cover 4 plates

½ cup chopped parsley (moss curled
  or Italian)

4 sliced hard-cooked eggs

8 black or green olives (optional)

Boil potatoes until soft. Remove from heat, mash immediately, and add cottage cheese, cumin, and salt. (If you wait until potatoes cool the mixture can become gooey.) Arrange lettuce leaves on 4 plates. When potato mixture has cooled to room temperature, scoop ½-cup portions onto lettuce. Sprinkle with goat cheese (if used) and parsley and arrange slices of hard-cooked eggs on top. Garnish with olives (if used).

For the ultimate touch, add a dollop of a fine-quality garlic mayonnaise.

SERVES 4.

Parsley Pesto

Margie Fromherz
Salem, Oregon

3 cups parsley leaves

3 or 4 cloves garlic

1 cup water

1 cup olive oil

¾ teaspoon salt

Pepper to taste

*2 tablespoons fresh rosemary or
1½ teaspoons dry*

*2 tablespoons fresh basil or 1 table-
spoon dry*

*2 tablespoons fresh oregano or
1½ teaspoons dry*

*2 tablespoons fresh thyme or
1½ teaspoons dry*

¾ cup Parmesan or Romano cheese

1½ pounds walnuts, coarsely ground

Combine everything but the cheese and nuts in a blender and process until smooth. Stir in cheese and nuts. Excellent over pasta, cooked grains, or in other dishes. May be divided and frozen for later use.

MAKES ABOUT 3 CUPS.

If you must dig parsnips for storage, keep them in sand or moist dirt in a cool place.

Parsnip Fritters

· ·

Nora Olson
Lorane, Oregon

4 or 5 parsnips

1 teaspoon flour

Salt

1 egg, beaten

Butter or beef drippings

Boil parsnips until tender, remove skins, and mash very fine. Add flour, salt, and beaten egg. Make the mixture into small cakes and fry them on both sides until golden brown. Serve very hot.

SERVES 4.

Pat's Squash Casserole

· ·

Pat Willis
Seattle, Washington

This is mega-cholesterol stuff but wonderful.

3 pounds good winter squash

1 can cream of chicken soup

1 large purple onion, diced

Handful chopped parsley

1 package herbed, bread stuffing mix
    (I use Pepperidge Farms)

1½ cups sour cream

Clean out squash and bake until barely soft to a poke with a fork. When it is cool enough to handle, peel and cut in 1-inch cubes. Stir squash into soup along with onion and parsley. Prepare stuffing mix per instructions on bag.

Layer the squash mixture, stuffing, and sour cream in a casserole in about 6 layers, ending with sour cream on top. Bake at 350°F for 45 minutes. Top should be brown.

SERVES 6 TO 8.

Potatogulasch

....

Paul Dreykus
Shelton, Washington

Easy and inexpensive, this is a filling dish from Vienna, Austria. I like to make large quantities that leave me free to work for a week or 10 days without cooking: just a warm-up for tasty meals.

Oil or cooking fat

1 large onion (about 1 pound)

6 large potatoes (about 4 pounds)

1 large clove garlic, crushed
   or minced

Salt and pepper

½ cup chopped parsley (optional)

Half a large green pepper, diced
   (optional)

Half a large red pepper, diced
   (optional)

2 stalks celery, diced, or ½ cup grated
   celeriac or 1 teaspoon celery seed

⅓ cup grated parsnip (optional)

1 tablespoon paprika

1 teaspoon caraway seed

Precooked sausage or diced ham

Judge how many portions you want to make by multiplying the usual size or quantity of potato you use per meal.

Use enough oil or cooking fat to moisten but not to float the onion. Stir in onion, parsley, peppers, celery or celeriac, and parsnip (if used) and cook over medium heat, stirring often, while you prepare the potatoes.

Peel potatoes and dice into ½-inch cubes. (I like to use 4-inch russets; any kind will turn out, but mealy potatoes that mush up are best and cook quicker, and large ones are less work.) When vegetables are almost done, turn up heat to brown them nicely. Watch carefully to avoid burning. Lower heat and add potatoes and just enough water to cover them. Add garlic, salt, pepper, paprika, caraway seed, and celery seed (if used). Cover and simmer gently, like rice. It will take about half an hour for potatoes to soften; check with a fork.

That's the finished treat for vegetarians and also for the poorest of the poor. The just poor used to add half-inch slices of garlic sausage, since that once was the cheapest meat. Now, as a delicatessen or designer specialty, it has been made into a luxury—if you can ever find garlic sausage at all.

Add just enough meat for the immediate meal about 10 minutes before the potatoes are done, or just after and let it simmer for 5 more minutes. Uncooked meat pieces can be added in proportion to the whole pot and cooked right along with the potatoes.

Later, when warming up servings, do add a little water and stir it in to prevent burning the bottom. Use low heat. Unless you have meat cooked in, add your measure of precooked meat for that meal.

Salad, pickles, sauerkraut, all go well with this goulasch, especially in summer, when it is hard to resist just eating it cold straight out of the pot. In winter, cooked kale and spinach are particularly fine with it.

SERVES 8.

!Quick! Stir-Fry

Lorretta Ward
Kotzebue, Alaska

⅔ cabbage

⅓ hamburger

No oil is needed

Fry hamburger and shredded cabbage together until meat is done and cabbage is crisp-tender. Add herbs or seasoning as you prefer or have on hand.

SERVES 1 OR MORE.

Pocket of Honey Squash

Donna Nelson
Nelson Farms, Brownsville, Oregon

1 golden acorn, acorn, or buttercup squash, about 5 inches diameter

Salt and pepper (optional)

2 tablespoons butter or margarine, divided

2 tablespoons brown sugar

2 tablespoons honey

Parsley and/or pineapple (optional)

Pumpkins and winter squash need warmish, dry conditions for storage. Don't put them in the basement with the potatoes and carrots. You will be told not to wash them before storage, but that isn't always practical if they are really dirty. I hose mine down, then cure them outside on a windy day if possible, and then bring them in for the winter. They are very decorative, especially if you have cut designs into them with a knife or a thumbnail before the shells harden in the field.

Different varieties have different keeping qualities. Pumpkins and Delicatas reach their peak of flavor after about a month, and then become progressively blander and stringier. Hubbards and Sweetmeats, on the other hand, will stay firm and sweet for months if cured properly.

Cut squash in two and remove seeds and strings. Place pieces, cut side down, in a microwave dish with a lid. Add 2 tablespoons water and microwave 6 to 8 minutes. Turn over to check for doneness (do not puncture skin) and microwave 2 minutes longer if necessary. Turn halves over and puncture flesh with a fork without breaking the skin. Add salt and pepper (if used). Put a tablespoon butter, a tablespoon brown sugar, and a tablespoon honey in each half. Return to microwave, cut side up, and cook 3 minutes more. Garnish if you like with fresh chopped parsley or sliced pineapple.

SERVE AS AN INDIVIDUAL VEGETABLE IN THE HALF OR PLACE ON PLATTER WITH A SPOON TO SERVE 4 TO 6.

Jamaican Meat-Stuffed Pumpkin

Donna Dreessen
Port Orchard, Washington

1 small Sweet Sugar Pumpkin (8 to 10 inches in diameter)

2 pounds lean ground beef

6 ounces ground ham

2½ cups finely chopped onion

1 green pepper, chopped

2½ teaspoons salt

1 teaspoon black pepper

2 teaspoons oregano

Shake red pepper flakes

1 teaspoon vinegar

¾ cup raisins

2 large cloves garlic (or powder)

1 can (8 ounces) tomato sauce

⅓ cup chopped pimiento-stuffed olives

3 eggs, beaten

Cut 5-inch top out of pumpkin. Save for lid. Scoop out seeds and scrape clean. Either place in microwave oven to bake until almost tender, or place in pan, cover with salted water, cover pan, and simmer until almost tender (about 30 minutes). Carefully remove and drain. Dry outside, and salt inside lightly. Sauté beef, ham, onions, and green pepper. Remove from heat and add salt, pepper, oregano, red pepper flakes, vinegar, and garlic. Add raisins, tomato sauce, and olives. Cover and cook over low heat for 15 minutes, stirring occasionally. Remove from heat, cool slightly, and add eggs, mixing thoroughly. Fill pumpkin, pressing stuffing slightly to pack it. Cover with lid. Place in shallow pan and bake at 350°F for one hour. Cool 15 minutes.

Cut in wedges to serve. Garnish with leaves or flowers if desired.

SERVES 8.

Pumpkin

· ·

Jennifer Mueller
Willamina, Oregon

There was a request on your order blank to enclose favorite recipes. I can't say these are exactly my favorite recipes (I think my favorite is for chocolate sweetheart pudding), but they are recipes I use. I can't exactly say they utilize fresh garden produce and healthful ingredients, either; they are basically harvest-time methods for dealing with surplus and they all require sugar. (My grandmother lived to be ninety and ate quantities of sugar every day of her life except during the two world wars, when it was rationed; I know a lot of people now think white sugar is poison, but with that example before me, I can't. She might have lived to be a hundred if she hadn't been subject to infections, and I never heard of sugar being connected with immune system deficiency, although I expect the present-day nutritional gestapo probably blames it for AIDS by now.)

While I use regular recipes for baking and so on, these are better suited to the touch method; they depend a good deal on the personal taste of the user and what is on hand to use. We don't have a year-round garden; at present writing the several inches of snow on the garden space is being removed by a hailstorm, and we have had frosts on the 21st of June and the 21st of September. I raise more green tomatoes than ripe ones. In fact, if it weren't for the green tomatoes, it wouldn't be worthwhile trying to raise ripe ones. When the freeze comes I take what green tomatoes I have on hand and use them. For that sort of cooking you need proportional recipes; so, assuming that my situation is not unique, I am providing what I can.

If you are making a pumpkin pie, for instance, how much pumpkin goes into the pie depends on how much you have, so you have to work on by guess and by gosh and personal taste—¼ cup of brown sugar to 1 cup pumpkin, perhaps, or ⅓ cup if you like it sweeter, or even ½ cup if your pumpkin needs more sweetening.

Which reminds me, I don't know if you know: When you fix your pumpkin, you may want to just put it in a casserole, with the inner pulp removed but the peel still on, put in a little water, and bake it until you can scrape the meat out of the skin. The same technique works with squash. Even if you do peel first, you should bake it, not boil it. Boiling leaves it full of water. Smash it up, add the sugar as suggested above, with about 1 teaspoon cornstarch per cup of pumpkin mixed into the sugar. Add your spices and there you are. Too many of the usual recipes are for pumpkin custard. Where the pioneers who made the first pumpkin pies got milk and eggs in the middle of winter no one seems to wonder. I will sometimes add a beaten egg or two, but milk just makes it sloppy. It also requires a measured amount of pumpkin, which means you will have pumpkin left over and it won't be enough to make another pie.

Saucy Brussels Sprouts

J. Yvonne Jones
Umpqua, Oregon

3 or 4 cups fresh Brussels sprouts

½ cup chopped onions

2 tablespoons butter

1 tablespoon flour

1 tablespoon brown sugar

1 teaspoon salt

½ teaspoon dry mustard

½ cup milk

1 cup sour cream

Wash and trim sprouts. Steam or boil in small amount of salted water for 10 to 15 minutes or until just tender. Drain. Meanwhile, in medium saucepan, cook onion in butter until tender but not brown. Stir in flour, brown sugar, salt, and mustard until blended. Stir in milk. Cook and stir until mixture thickens and bubbles. Blend in sour cream. (Don't boil after adding sour cream.) Add sprouts and stir gently to combine.

SERVES 6 TO 8.

Stir-Fry Curried Cabbage

·····································

Debbie Stevens
Bonney Lake, Washington

¼ cup butter or margarine

½ cabbage head (sliced thin)

½ to ¾ teaspoon curry powder

Pepper to taste

Melt butter or margarine in non-stick fry pan over medium heat. Add cabbage. Stir and cook 1 minute. Add curry powder and pepper. Continue cooking until tender but still crisp.

SERVES 5 OR 6.

Winter Squash Casserole

·····································

Nora Olson
Lorane, Oregon

2 pounds winter squash

1 medium onion, chopped

Half a green pepper, chopped

1½ tablespoons melted butter

2 eggs, beaten

¾ cup cracker crumbs

½ cup grated American cheese

Salt, pepper, and garlic salt to taste

Slice squash and add onion and green pepper. Cook in water until squash is tender.

Preheat oven to 350°F. Drain squash and add butter, eggs, and cracker crumbs. Mix well, put into greased dish, and top with cheese. Bake 50 minutes.

SERVES 4 OR 5.

Beet Cake

....

Stella Markee
Tillamook, Oregon

1¾ cups flour

1½ teaspoons soda

¼ teaspoon salt

1½ cups sugar

3 eggs

1 cup oil

1½ cups grated cooked beets

2 to 4 tablespoons cocoa

½ teaspoon vanilla

Preheat oven to 350°F. Mix flour, soda, salt, sugar, and cocoa together and set aside. Beat together eggs and oil. Add vanilla and beat well. Add dry ingredients, beat well, and then stir in beets. Pour into a lightly greased cake pan and bake 30 to 35 minutes.

Editor's Note: This combination of beets and chocolate was news to me, but I've since learned that it is well known to Dutch cooks. It makes a moist, dark, delicious cake. Canned (not pickled) beets can be substituted for fresh cooked.

MAKES ONE 2-LAYER ROUND
CAKE OR SINGLE-LAYER
RECTANGULAR CAKE.

Carrot Cake

Marian Glenz
Meyers Chuck, Alaska

2 cups flour

1½ cups sugar

2 teaspoons cinnamon

1 teaspoon baking soda

Salt

¾ cup milk

2 eggs

½ cup oil

2 teaspoons vanilla

2 cups finely chopped carrots

1 can (8 ounces) crushed pineapple

1 cup chopped nuts

Preheat oven to 350°F. Combine dry ingredients. Beat in milk, eggs, oil, and vanilla. Stir in carrots, pineapple, and nuts. Bake until springy, about 30 minutes. No frosting is necessary.

1 RECTANGULAR CAKE.

Radishes make a good nurse crop for slow-germinating seeds like carrots and parsnips. They mark the row, keep the soil from crusting over, and also shade the soil around the vulnerable young plants.

Mock Mincemeat Pie

....

Phyllis Michelson
Ridgefield, Washington

Tastes and smells like real mincemeat pie.

2 apples, chopped

2 green tomatoes, chopped

1 cup sugar

½ cup raisins

1 tablespoon margarine

1 teaspoon cinnamon

1 teaspoon nutmeg

½ teaspoon cloves

½ teaspoon salt

Pastry for double-crust 9-inch pie

Preheat oven to 425°F. Mix everything together in a saucepan, bring to a boil, and cook 5 minutes. Pour into pastry shell. Top with remaining pastry and bake.

MAKES ONE 9-INCH PIE.

Laura Ingalls Wilder's Green Pumpkin Pie

Jennifer Mueller
Willamina, Oregon

You will find the original for this in *The Long Winter*, where it was actually devised by Mrs. Ingalls, Laura's mother.

"Laura, you go to the cornpatch and bring me a green pumpkin. I'm going to make a pie!"

"A pie! But how...." Mary said, and Laura said, "A green pumpkin pie? I never heard of such a thing, Ma."

"Neither did I," said Ma. "But we wouldn't do much if we didn't do things that nobody ever heard of before."

...Laura ran through the cool, misty rain and lugged back the biggest green pumpkin... "Now what do I do?"

"You may cut the pumpkin in slices and peel them while I make the piecrust," said Ma. "Then we'll see what we'll see."

Ma put the crust in the pie pan and covered the bottom with brown sugar and spices. Then she filled the crust with thin slices of the green pumpkin. She poured half a cup of vinegar over them, put a small piece of butter on top, and laid the top crust over all.

"There," she said when she had finished crimping the edges.

"I didn't know you could," Carrie breathed, looking wide-eyed at the pie.

"Well, I don't know yet," said Ma. She slipped the pie into the oven and shut the door on it. "But the only way to find out is to try. By dinnertime we'll know."

Just before dinnertime Ma took the pie from the oven. It was a beautiful pie.

They kept dinner waiting until almost one o'clock, but Pa did not come... So at last they ate dinner. The pie must wait until suppertime...

For an instant Pa did not see it. Then he said, "Pie!... However did you manage to make a pie? What kind of pie is it?"

"Taste it and see!" said Ma.

Pa cut off the point with his fork. "Apple pie! Where in the world did you get apples?"

Carrie could keep still no longer. She almost shouted, "It's pumpkin! Ma made it of green pumpkin!"

Pa took another small bit. "I'd never have guessed it," he said. "Ma always could beat the nation cooking."

—*The Long Winter*
(Harper & Row, 1971), pp. 33-35

Ma's pie is really not that much like an apple pie unless you have been a long time without apple pie, but it is still a very good pie and well worth making if pie materials are scarce to nonexistent (as they were for the Ingalls) or even if they aren't and you would like a different kind of pie, or just if an early freeze has left you with a nice green pumpkin.

Cut your pumpkin in wedges, cut off the inner pulp and immature seeds (as one assumes Laura did, even though it is not mentioned), and slice the wedges thinly across. A sugar pumpkin fills a small pie, a Halloween pumpkin needs a larger pie, or two pies.

Use ¾ cup brown sugar; Ma sprinkled it on the bottom, but I reserve a bit for the top as well.

Sprinkle cinnamon or apple pie spice over the sugar. Put the pumpkin on the sugar and pour on ⅓ cup fresh or reconstituted lemon juice. Ma was probably using a teacup, not a measuring cup; her vinegar was probably milder than ours, and certainly not distilled.

The first time I made the pie, it was not very successful and certainly not as described. I had baked it the standard pie time and heat— 40 minutes at 400°F. The pumpkin slices were still hard and tasteless, the juice a thin syrup. So I went back and read the account over. I realized, then, that Ma would never waste fuel to bake a very experimental pie! She was using a range, and the pie cooked in the heat from the firebox. Her oven was probably around 300°F, and the pie baked from about nine in the morning until noon, and she turned the pie so that it would brown evenly. So I tried that. It made an elegant pie; the pumpkin was soft and had soaked up all the juice and flavor. So profit by my experience and don't try to bake it like a regular pie.

As may be deduced from the above, it is an excellent pie to make if you do have a wood or coal range and don't want to go to any special lengths to heat up the oven.

Persimmon Cake

Norma Dolowitz Giddings
Petaluma, California

I submitted this because I've found that persimmons are difficult to find many things to do with, and this is wonderful tasting. It freezes well.

2 cups persimmon pulp

2 cups sugar

2 tablespoons oil

2 cups chopped walnuts

2 cups raisins

3 cups flour (could be half whole wheat or whole wheat pastry)

½ teaspoon cloves

2 teaspoons cinnamon

1 teaspoon salt

2 teaspoons baking soda

Preheat oven to 325°F. Mix together persimmon pulp, sugar, oil, walnuts, and raisins and set aside. Combine flour, cloves, cinnamon, salt, and baking soda and add to persimmon mixture. Pour in greased bundt pan or 2 medium loaf pans and bake 1½ hours.

MAKES 1 BUNDT CAKE OR 2 MEDIUM LOAVES.

Extraneous Wines or By-Product Beverages

Jennifer Mueller
Willamina, Oregon

Wine can be made from a lot of things. It can even be made from a lot of things you would otherwise throw away. You do throw them away after making the wine from them, of course, but this does give them a second use. Wine-making is an organic business, not like baking a cake, so the quantities can vary a bit. The technique is more important. I devised this recipe on noticing that root wine recipes called for grated carrots, parsnips, turnips, etc. I realized why grate a good vegetable when there are all those peels? Don't worry about the peels possibly having dirt on them. The boiling kills bacteria and the silt sticks on the bottom, which is why you siphon the wine.

ROOT WINE

Specifically, carrot. When you fix your carrots for freezing, take off the tops and keep them separate from the peels. When you are finished freezing, take the peels and boil them 15 to 20 minutes or more in the water left in the kettle. If you changed the water during your freezing, save the first lot and put it back in. Strain your peels out and you will be left with carrot infusion. It helps to have something like a small cider press to get the wine out of the mash, but it isn't absolutely necessary. With luck you'll have about 3 quarts,

which goes nicely in a gallon jar. If you did a lot of freezing, you will have about 7 quarts and will have to use a 2-gallon crock or two 1-gallon jars.

Start each gallon jar with 2 cups sugar and about ½ can frozen orange juice. If the water is still hot when you put in the sugar, it will help it dissolve. If the water is still cold after thawing the orange juice, it will kill the yeast. So wait until the liquid is about room temperature and then sprinkle yeast on top. It doesn't take much.

You will also need one shredded-wheat biscuit or a cup of cracked wheat or a slice of whole wheat toast. This can be added to the liquid, in which case it will eventually have to be strained out, or boiled with the carrot peels and strained out with them, although I cannot attest to the efficacy of this in all cases. At any rate, all root wines seem to require wheat in some form. You have to strain the particles out of the orange juice, too.

Any wine with solids in it needs to be stirred once a day. Once the wine is working, add about ½ cup sugar every other day or so. Five to 10 peppercorns add flavor. Keep wine covered or you will get fruit flies and other nonsense in it, which can mean—vinegar!

At the end of two weeks, strain through three layers of cheesecloth if wine needs straining. Taste the wine two days before it is due to be bottled, so if it needs more sugar you can add it then, which will give the wine time to settle again before it is bottled. If you strain your wine, let it sit for two days afterwards to settle. Once settled, wine is siphoned off into well-washed bottles and sealed. You don't have to sterilize your bottles, and if you wash them as soon as

they are empty, further cleaning need be no more than a rinse to remove dust.

Seal your bottles with corks. Yes, I know commercial wines use screw caps, but they are pasteurized and have stopped working. Boil your cork to soften it and wiggle it as best you can; you only need to protect the wine from air. The basic principle is that the cork should blow out before the bottle blows up.

This is good for the aforesaid carrots, parsnips, turnips, and rutabaga, I would assume, though I have not attempted the last. Beets you boil and then freeze after slipping the peels off, so just put the slipped-off peels back in the boiling water and proceed as before. If you want red beet wine, you have to exclude all light; use a crock with a plate on top, and very dark glass bottles. Beet wine is excellent combined with raspberry (see below).

FRUIT WINE

Specifically, raspberry. If you don't like seeds in your teeth you make jelly. Take the seeds and skins left after straining and add water equal to the amount of juice that was poured off. Note: If your water is chlorinated, boil it first or let it stand overnight. Chlorine will kill your yeast. Add whatever juice is left over from your jelly recipe, pan scrapings if you have them, etc. Use a cup of sugar for each quart of liquid. Proceed as for root wines, stirring every day. It's best to use a straight-sided container; if the wine is restricted at the top it may work up and overflow. Taste every so often, especially before bottling, as this is best sweet. You can use raspberries, blackberries, red currants, overripe plums, peach skins, and parts of overripe peach as well, grape mash, etc. Not apples, not pears. Not elderberries, either. This doesn't need wheat or orange juice, but can be combined nicely with the root wines above: raspberry-beet, carrot-peach, etc.

White vinegar makes excellent pickles if you are into pickling.

Did you enjoy this book?

Sasquatch Books publishes books and guides related to the Pacific Northwest. Our books are available at bookstores and other retail outlets throughout the region. Here is a selection of our current titles:

COOKBOOKS

Breakfast in Bed
The Best B&B Recipes from Northern California, Oregon, Washington, and British Columbia
Carol Frieberg

Eight Items or Less Cookbook
Fine Food in a Hurry
Ann Lovejoy

Winter Harvest Cookbook
How to Select and Prepare Fresh Seasonal Produce All Winter Long
Lane Morgan

TRAVEL

Northwest Best Places
Restaurants, Lodgings, and Touring in Oregon, Washington, and British Columbia
David Brewster and Stephanie Irving

Portland Best Places
A Discriminating Guide to Portland's Restaurants, Lodgings, Shopping, Nightlife, Arts, Sights, Outings, and Annual Events
Stephanie Irving

Seattle Best Places
A Discriminating Guide to Seattle's Restaurants, Lodgings, Shopping, Nightlife, Arts, Sights, Outings, and Annual Events
David Brewster and Stephanie Irving

Seattle Cheap Eats
300 Terrific Bargain Eateries
Kathryn Robinson and Stephanie Irving

GARDENING

The Border in Bloom
A Northwest Garden Through the Seasons
Ann Lovejoy

Gardening Under Cover
A Northwest Guide to Solar Greenhouses, Cold Frames, and Cloches
William Head

Growing Vegetables West of the Cascades
Steve Solomon's Complete Guide to Natural Gardening
3rd edition

Three Years in Bloom
A Garden-Keeper's Journal
Introduction by Ann Lovejoy

Trees of Seattle
The Complete Tree-finder's Guide to 740 Varieties
Arthur Lee Jacobson

Winter Gardening in the Maritime Northwest
Cool Season Crops for the Year-Round Gardener
Binda Colebrook, 3rd edition

The Year in Bloom
Gardening for All Seasons in the Pacific Northwest
Ann Lovejoy

To receive a Sasquatch Books catalog, or to inquire about ordering our books by phone or mail, please contact us at the address below.

SASQUATCH BOOKS
1931 Second Avenue
Seattle, WA 98101
(206) 441-5555